180 DAYS OF **BEAUTIFUL** TRUTH

When You Change Your Mind,
You Change Your Life

SPARKLE R. SANDERS

Scripture quotations marked NLT are taken from the Holy Bible, New Living Translation, copyright 1996, 2004, 2007. Used by permission of Tyndale House Publishers, Inc. Carol Stream, Illinois 60188. All rights reserved. Scripture quotations marked NIV are taken from the Holy Bible, New International Version. NIV. Copyright 1973, 1978, 1984 by International Bible Society. Used by permission of Zondervan. All rights reserved.

ISBN: 978-1-4834-6613-2 (sc)
ISBN: 978-1-4834-6614-9 (e)

Library of Congress Control Number: 2017902867

Lulu Publishing Services rev. date: 10/16/2017

Dedications

I dedicate this book to:

My Lord and Savior Jesus Christ. I am nothing without You. Thank you for saving me from darkness and pulling me into your marvelous light. Every hurt and pain You've allowed me to go through and overcome has led me to write this book and share my wisdom with others. Thank you, Lord.

My husband for your unconditional love and unending support. Thank you for always inspiring, challenging, and encouraging me to be the best woman I can be. I wouldn't be here and be the woman I am today without you. I love you.

My family and friends. Thank you for always loving me and allowing me to be myself. You push me to be "me" and nothing else. I thank God for you!

Every person who has ever felt rejected, unloved, unappreciated, unrecognized, heartbroken, abandoned, confused, depressed, destroyed, and the like. I know and have experienced the same pain. You're the inspiration for this book and for carrying out God's will for my life. This book is for you.

"Do not be conformed by the patterns of this world. But be transformed by the renewing of your mind. Then, you will be able to test and approve what God's will is for you. His good, pleasing and perfect will." Romans 12:2

Day 1

You're not the same man or woman you used to be. God has changed you. He's transformed you from the inside out. Today, receive the change God has given you. Don't act like it didn't happen because you see fragments of your old nature resurfacing. Just because you see that old behavior doesn't mean the change you received wasn't real. It doesn't mean God didn't deliver or change you. That "old self" you see creeping back up isn't the real you. That's never who God intended for you to be. Those actions, feelings, and thought processes have been destroyed. They're gone. But you must believe they're gone. You must have faith that God did what He said He would do. It's by faith you walk, not by sight. Quit allowing what you see to trick and deceive you, to make you think you haven't been renewed. That's a lie from the enemy. God saved you and it's a done deal. When you accepted Him in your heart and confessed Jesus as Lord, it was sealed. It can't be changed. But your mind, will, and emotions still need to be transformed. They still need to line up with God's word and His original design for you. That's the part He is still working to renew. Let Him work. Let Him transform your thoughts and actions to be more like Him. You can't change them on your own. Just keep your heart and eyes fixed on Jesus. He will do the rest.

**Truth Verses: 2 Corinthians 5:17, Ezekiel 36:26,
2 Corinthians 5:7, Hebrews 12:2**

Beautiful Truth

Day 2

And there is nothing wrong with you. You're fearfully and wonderfully made. Today, quit going through your list of flaws to God. He made you. He designed everything in you. He knows how you are. You don't need to complain to Him about how you mess up in certain areas or how you can't get something right. You're looking at yourself through muddled glasses. But you're not your judge or anyone else's. God is. And He sees none of what you see when He looks at you. God only sees His precious child, His beloved. He only sees how wonderful you are, how much He loves you and how He can take your flaws and use them for His good. Stop looking so negatively at yourself. Nobody enjoys being around someone with low self-esteem. Sure, you're not perfect and you have areas to grow in. But what about your strengths? What about the things you do well? Focus on that. Write them down and say them aloud daily. Quit seeing yourself only through what you can't do. You can do all things through Christ who gives you strength. You're the head and not the tail. You're above only, never beneath. That's who you are in Christ Jesus, not those disheartening things people have or you have said about yourself. You're the righteousness of God in Christ. Remember that.

**Truth Verses: Psalm 139:14, Deuteronomy 28:13,
Song of Solomon 4:7, 2 Corinthians 5:21**

Beautiful Truth

Day 3

No pain, no gain. Today, it may not feel like it, but it's in your pain you prosper. It's in your suffering, heartache, and dark days that you grow and develop. You become stronger through them. You become better. You become all that God has created you to be. You can't get that type of growth from easy and comfortable times. Only hard times stretch you. Only challenging situations bring you to your knees and draw you closer to God. Quit feeling bad about them. Sure, you're in a difficult circumstance. Yes, what you're going through is no laughing matter. But if there weren't any good in it and if it was going to break you, God wouldn't allow it. He wouldn't let you to go through any of this if He wasn't going to protect you. Why? Because He is your Provider and Redeemer. He is your God in whom you trust. He loves you. He's not going to let you slip or fall. He's not going to let this circumstance take you out. Nobody is discrediting the challenge you're facing. But start looking at it differently. See God's mighty hand in it. See how He's keeping you. See how He's shielding, leading and guiding you despite it. No, God is not the cause of your problem or the one to blame. He is a good and gracious God always. But He doesn't waste a hurt. He will not waste a single tear you've shed or any pain you've felt. He's going to bless you right through it. Remember that as you go forth today.

**Truth Verses: Romans 8:28, Galatians 6:9,
2 Corinthians 4:8 – 9, Psalm 34:18**

Beautiful Truth

Day 4

And yes, you do have a voice in this world. You have a testimony. You have plenty to say and share with others. Today, quit letting the enemy silence you. The things you've been through should've broken you. They should've destroyed you. They should've killed you. You shouldn't even be here right now. But God. He saved you. He favored you. He delivered, protected, and blessed you. How dare you sit back and say nothing at all about what He's done? How dare you sit back and not shout it from the rooftops that your God has changed and transformed you? Your Father has been good to you. Tell somebody about it. Someone needs to hear your story. Someone needs to know what you've been through. Someone needs to know it hasn't always been a bed of roses for you. Someone needs to know how God set you free. Why? Because they need your encouragement. They need to know God is still for them and hasn't forgotten them. They need to know He still hears them. Quit keeping your mouth closed. Allow God to use you today. Let Him use your story and what you've been through to heal and provide comfort to others.

Truth Verses: Revelation 12:11, Mark 5:19, Isaiah 49:15 – 16

Beautiful Truth

Day 5

And you call on everyone else. But are you calling on the name of the Lord? Today, God is your deliverer. He is your refuge and stronghold in times of trouble, not anyone else. Yes, your family and friends are great. Sure, your pastor is wonderful. But nobody can take care of you like God can. Nobody can heal, comfort, and love you like He can. Jesus died so that you may live. He sacrificed His life so you could walk free in yours. His sacrifice allows you to walk in abundance, peace and joy on this earth. Learn how to accept that. How? Turn your heart towards Him. Seek Him for help. Humble yourself and ask Him for guidance. Quit running around to everyone else looking for the answer. Stop looking to your colleagues and friends for the solution. Stop looking to the news and media. Stop seeking the world for their hand. Seek Jesus' hand. He is the answer. He is the way, truth, and life. No, you may not be able to physically see Him, or reach out and touch Him like you can others. But that doesn't make Him any less powerful or real in your life. He is still right here with you, watching over you and waiting to help you. Don't continue to leave Him out. Invite Him in so you can experience real change in your life.

Truth Verses: Psalm 18:2, John 10:10, 1 Chronicles 16:11, John 14:6

Day 6

Today, if you want the best, then trust God to give you the best. Quit settling for the breadcrumbs of life. That's the world's way of doing things. That's the world's mentality and answer to unhappiness and discontentment. But it's not God's. God said He supplies all your needs according to His riches and glory. He said delight yourself in Him and He will give you the desires of your heart. Seeing your prayers answered has nothing to do with just "getting by." It has nothing to do with you proving something to this world and satisfying what they think you should have. Too many times you are just seconds away from the very thing you're believing God for, but you get impatient. You get thrown off because people are in your ear, telling you that you want too much or that God won't come through. Or that what you believe for is too big or too much. But the truth is everyone can't handle what you're believing and asking God for. They don't have faith as small as a mustard seed or understand the dream God has placed in your heart. So, stop telling them. They only speak and see your God in a small way. But you see differently. You see Him as a great God, a strong and mighty warrior. You see Him as the Kings of Kings and the Lord of Lords. You see His supply as endless. You see His resources as unlimited. Keep doing so. Don't just settle for the "leftovers" of life with God. He isn't a liar. Ask and keep asking according to His will. And you will receive everything you are asking for. Remember that.

Truth Verses: Philippians 4:19, Psalm 37:4, Matthew 17:20, Matthew 7:7

Beautiful Truth

Day 7

And it's not that God is distant. You just can't hear or see Him with all the drama you have going on around you. Today, you can't feed on junk and expect to be close to God. God is holy and pure. He's righteous, full of peace and joy. There isn't mess and chaos around Him. There isn't any "he said, she said." There isn't any backbiting, lies, and deceit. There's no darkness in God. Those things are from the enemy. He places those things in your life, but you're the one accepting them. God never intended for your life to be full of mess. You're not supposed to feel mixed up and confused all the time. You're not supposed to feel betrayed and like you can't trust anyone. You're not supposed to feel depressed, down and out all the time. Take a look at what's around you. Who are you spending your time with? Who and what are you listening to? What are you seeing and thinking about? You can't ponder on the mess of this world yet still draw near to God. It's a contradiction. The fear and worry of the world will drown out the peace and love of God if that's what you're paying the most attention to. Clean out the clutter in your life. Stop looking at and listening to the drama-filled things in your world. Turn off the news. Shut off the phone. Cut out the depressing, draining conversations. Take that time and energy to spend with the Lord. Get into His Word. Speak with Him. Sing songs to Him. Get into His presence. You have to eliminate the drama to receive and see the peace of the Lord. You must feed more on Him than anything else. Remember that.

Truth Verses: James 4:8, Philippians 4:8, Colossians 3:2

Beautiful Truth

Day 8

And everybody has gone through something. You're not the only one. That's why God placed certain people in your life to be there when you need. Today, you're not alone. Quit letting the enemy make you believe that. He's good at making you feel like nobody understands how you feel. He's good at making you feel left out and not a part of "the crowd". He wants you to feel isolated and like nobody can relate to you. But that's not true. Of all the people in this world and all the people God has placed in your life, you honestly think He created nobody to fit you? You honestly believe nobody "gets" you or can connect with you? Stop it. God always provides what you need, including companionship. He created you to connect with and delight in others. Quit being so closed off. Yes, you have some challenges and difficulties. But other people do too. They've gone through similar hurts and pains. Because of that, they can understand how you feel. They can relate to you. They can keep you encouraged and motivated during these trying times. Open yourself up to others. Stop thinking you're supposed to deal with your problems all on your own. God always raises someone up to be in your corner when you need it. But you have to let them in.

Truth Verses: Isaiah 41:10, Ecclesiastes 4: 9 – 10, Genesis 2:18, Matthew 18:20

Beautiful Truth

Day 9

And just because you want this season and time in your life to be over doesn't mean it will be. Today, nothing is over until God says it's over. As painful as it is, stand still and wait on the Lord. You're in control of nothing. You're on God's time, not your own. Yes, God takes your wants and desires into account. He listens to you when you cry out to Him. But just because you cry out and want something doesn't mean you're going to get it. Why? Because if it's going to hurt or destroy you, God will not allow it. That's how much He loves you. If you're in His will, He'll let nothing destroy or take you out. The Word says no "good" thing does He withhold from you. So, if it were good for you to be out of this season, you would be. But since you're not, there's still something you need to see. There's still some wisdom you need to receive. There's still some selfish desires and old habits that need to die. There's still some relationships and people you need to break away from. Quit thinking this season is a punishment from God. This season is about teaching you something. It's a life lesson. It's discipline. And God teaches and disciplines those He loves because He wants the best for them. Trust that He wants the best for you today. Instead of fighting Him, work with Him. Allow Him to use these circumstances to refresh and restore you, to turn it around for your good. Allow Him to change your thinking and do a new thing in your life. You keep talking about how much you want a change. Well, this is the way. Your job isn't to judge or like it. It's to trust God through it.

**Truth Verses: Psalm 46:10, Isaiah 48:17, Psalm 84:11,
Proverbs 3:12, Jeremiah 31:25**

Beautiful Truth

Day 10

As bad as it is for you right now, there's always someone worse off. Today, be thankful for what you do have, even during hard times. Nobody is saying that what you're going through isn't tragic. Nobody is saying that it isn't difficult or it isn't affecting you. But it's all about perspective. That's what God is always trying to show you. You complain about the item you can't afford to buy, but at least you do have some money in your pocket. You complain about the car breaking down, but at least you have one to drive. You complain about the minor aches and pains you get, but at least it's not a terminal illness. It's all about how you see it. Too many times you let the enemy get into your head and blow issues out of portion. Yes, there's problems in your life. But it's nothing your Father can't fix. It's nothing that He's not going to give you the grace to handle. The Word promises that nothing by no means shall hurt and harm you. These battles and challenges of life will come, but they're not going to destroy you. They are hard and uncomfortable, but they aren't going to take you out.

Don't let setbacks get you into ungratefulness and bitterness today. Things may not be going the way you want them to, but it's ok. Hold your head high. God has an ultimate plan. In the meantime, continue to thank Him for what you do have. Take that complaining, negative energy and turn it into prayers for others who are in more challenging situations than you are.

**Truth Verses: 1 Thessalonians 5:18, Luke 10:19,
Isaiah 54:17, Philippians 2:14**

Beautiful Truth

Day 11

The promises of God are "yes" and "amen." All you have to do is believe it. Today, how much do you really believe? Too many times you quote scriptures and the things of God, but you don't truly believe it. It sounds good. You sound righteous and holy saying it, but your heart isn't in it. You're mouthing the words, but the truth is your heart is full of doubt and unbelief. You've been let down and disappointed for so long, you no longer believe that God is going to come through. But He is. God is still God. He made you a promise. And He won't change that for any circumstance, place, person, or thing. He is still good, faithful, and true. And just because you're going through a rough patch it doesn't mean He's changed His mind about you. He's not going back on His promises for your life. Your current situation isn't a concern to God. He loves you. He wants to bless and provide for you. Yes, you feel worn out and weary. But those who hope in the Lord will renew their strength. Ask God to renew your strength in Him today. Ask Him to give you the courage to believe in His promises. Then and only then will you have the faith you need to keep going and finish strong in your race.

Truth Verses: 2 Corinthians 1:20, Hebrews 10:23, Isaiah 40:31, Hebrews 12:1

Beautiful Truth

Day 12

And no matter how crazy your life gets God keeps looking out for you. Today, praise God for that alone. You will go through periods in your life where you will feel like nothing makes sense, like everything and everyone is against you. But in all that, God is still looking out for you. He is keeping you. He still has your best interest at heart. In the midst of your circumstance today, don't forget that. Too many times you get wrapped up in your feelings. You allow the enemy to make you feel so bad about the situation and what's happening that you forget your stance in God. You forget He's above it all. You forget He's bigger and mightier than any situation or problem. And that's when you become defeated and depressed. That's when you give in to the lies of the enemy. Stop it. God is in control of your situation. Craziness and chaos can't overtake you. Sickness can't over take you. Lack can't over take you. Hopelessness can't over take you. You're more than a conqueror. Fight through the drama you see today. Fight through your feelings and the pettiness. These things are only there to distract and keep your focus off the things of God. Don't fall for the trick. Keep your eyes on Jesus. Have confidence and faith in Him, not in what's going on around you.

**Truth Verses: Genesis 28:15, Psalm 16:8, Romans 8:37,
Hebrews 12:2**

Beautiful Truth

Day 13

And you're not blessed because your spouse is cute, your car is fancy, or your house is big. You're blessed because God is with you. Today, quit seeking attention from this world and calling it "blessed". Blessed is a constant state. You were born blessed. Blessed doesn't care how much money you have in your pocket or how many bedrooms are in your house. Blessed isn't concerned with how many "likes" your social media posts get or how many people comment on your photo. Blessed isn't out to feed your self-esteem or get approvals. Blessed is who you are every day. It's what God declared over you when you were in your mother's womb. It's who you are when you're in an apartment or a mansion. It's who you are when you're on vacation or when you can't afford one. It's who you are when you're single or when you're in a relationship. It's who you are if you live in a big city or small town. Quit thinking it's something else. Yes, God blesses all of us with wonderful possessions. But it's because of His goodness and unconditional love. It's not because of your looks, smarts, or wits. It's not because you went to college or because of your family name. God is good to you all the time because He wants to be. That's the true blessing – that no matter what situation you find yourself in God is taking care of you. Remember that.

Truth Verses: Psalm 46:7, Numbers 6:24 – 26,
Deuteronomy 28: 3 – 6, 1 Corinthians 15:10

Beautiful Truth

Day 14

And if you can't even enjoy where you are now, how do you expect to enjoy where God is taking you? Today, be content in all circumstances. Too many times you think you need to wait until the situation changes before you can be happy, or have peace and joy. But joy and peace don't work like that. They are not circumstantial. They don't depend on how you feel or what you think should happen. When Jesus died for you, He didn't make your peace and joy conditional. He didn't die so that you can you feel peace only when the situation called for it. He said in all things, have peace. He said in all things, count it joy. Yes, it's hard. Sure, it's difficult to smile and laugh when you're feeling disappointed. But God isn't asking you to force a smile or laugh. He isn't asking you to be fake. He's asking you to know in your heart that He's got you, that He's not going to let you fall or slip. That's where true contentment comes from. It's a knowing in your heart. It's confidence in your God. It's confidence in His grace, mercies and promises. Stop looking for contentment from your emotions and feelings. Look to God's faithfulness and goodness. Then, you'll begin to experience the true peace that surpasses all understanding.

Truth Verses: Philippians 4:11 – 12, James 1:2, Philippians 4:7

Day 15

And it's easy to want to fix "it." But the truth is some things you have no control over. The only way they'll get fixed is through God. Today, recognize that. Without God in it, you're powerless. You're nothing more than a hamster on a hamster wheel. You can try all the ideas, tricks, and schemes you want. And you'll stress yourself out doing so. Learn how to tap into the presence of the Lord. Sit at His feet. Go before Him in prayer, tell Him your desires. Believe Him to supply all of your needs. Everything you need is already complete in Jesus. Can you stop trying to force it, but allow God to manifest it? That's what His grace and walking by faith truly is. It's not knowing all the details. It's not "rubbing elbows" with who you know to get you somewhere. It's not "name-dropping". It's trusting and believing God. It's believing that even when you've tried, even when you don't have any more answers or solutions, even when it looks like the cards are stacked up against you, God knows what's best. You're the righteousness of God in Christ. You don't have to fix your own problems. God's your Good Shepherd and He's taking care of all areas of your life. Remember that.

Truth Verses: Matthew 11:28 – 30, John 19:30, John 11:40, Psalm 23:1

Beautiful Truth

Day 16

God delivered you from the situation because it was no good for you. It wasn't His best. But you want to go back. Today, stop being like the Israelites. Stop desiring to go back to a season in your life that you know was wrong only because you don't love where you are right now. Life is a journey. Every season in your life you're not going to love. But just because it's different and unfamiliar doesn't mean you go running back to the old and comfortable. The enemy is deceiving you. He's making you feel like your past was better than it truly was. When he's showing you all the wonderful memories in your head and what "could've" been, he fails to highlight the bad days, and all the hurt and the pain. He fails to show you how lost, confused and miserable you were. Don't negate that. Don't let the enemy fill your head with this deception making you think you're missing the "good ol' days." You're not. Christ saved and delivered you from the evil and darkness you were in because it was harmful. God had a greater plan for your life than the mess you were in. And that's where you are now. Stay with it. It is right where God's will for your life needs you to be.

**Truth Verses: Philippians 3:14, Jeremiah 29:11,
1 Peter 2:9, Deuteronomy 4:20**

Beautiful Truth

Day 17

If someone didn't choose you, that's not your fault. That's what they decided. It's not on you. Today, quit taking the rejection personal. The enemy is good at making you feel like you did something wrong. He's good at making you feel like you didn't care enough, love enough, do enough, or work hard enough to keep someone in your good graces. But the truth is no matter how hard you tried if they weren't meant to stay in your life, nothing you did would've made a difference. Even if they or you, would've changed, it still wouldn't have been enough. It just wasn't meant for that person to be in your life forever. They were only meant to be there throughout certain seasons of your life. There's no room for them in your future. That's why they had to reject you. That's why they had to abandon you. They may not even realize why they were doing it. But it was God ordained. It was never about you personally. It was about where God is taking you. They can't be a part of that. Their character isn't equipped for that. God needs you connected to people who are growing and transforming as you are. Stop being upset about the people who left or didn't love you. Whether it was platonic or intimate, God wants you to stop blaming yourself. There's nothing wrong with you as a person. All you did was be yourself. And there's nothing wrong with that. You're God's beloved, fearfully and wonderfully made. You're more than the rejection you experienced and hurt you felt. You're His precious child. Never forget that.

Truth Verses: Psalm 118:22, 1 Peter 2:4, Romans 8:1, Song of Solomon 6:3

Beautiful Truth

Day 18

And the trial is not supposed to crush you. It's supposed to grow you. Today, what are you learning from the difficult situation you're in? Or are you just complaining about it? The truth is life will not always be "peaches and cream." Every day you won't "tip through the tulips." But just because the situation is challenging doesn't mean you conform to it by walking in frustration, defeat or self-pity. Yes, it's not what you expected or even wanted. But go through it with the right attitude. Go through it knowing God is for you, with you and loves you. God never said just because you serve and praise Him that you'd never have another hard day in your life. He never said your walk and journey in this life was going to be easy. He told you there would be persecution, heartache, and pain. He said enemies would rise against you. But with Christ, you can do all things. In Him, you have the peace that surpasses all understanding. That's what God is trying to teach you in this situation. That's what He's trying to teach you for life. Learn it. Absorb it. Walk in it. Learning how to remain joyful and at peace through trials isn't a test you're supposed to pass and then forget. It's God's life lesson to you. But if you keep letting everything that comes your way pull and tug at you, you'll never learn the lesson. You'll continue to be the enemy's puppet, and he'll pull your strings forever. Remember that.

Truth Verses: John 16:33, 1 Peter 4: 12 – 13, Psalm 16:11, Psalm 62:8

Beautiful Truth

Day 19

And here's why worrying does you no good: because no matter what the outcome is, you're going to be just fine. God has your back regardless. Today, when your mind starts racing, remember that. So many times you play right into the enemy's hand by just not thinking at all. How is a God who has looked out for you all this time suddenly going to just let you fall? How is a God who has brought you through the darkness, who comforted, healed and delivered you, now just suddenly going to drop you? He's not. That's a lie from the enemy. Just because the outcome you want has not been the one you received doesn't mean God isn't still God. It just means He hasn't always catered to your preference. And that's what scares you. You think it will be more miserable if the situation doesn't turn out your way. But "your way" may not be the best way. Because of that, don't focus on "your way". Just focus on God. Focus on His love for you. Focus on His faithfulness. Some way, somehow He's always provided for you. He's always gotten you what you needed when you needed it. Continue letting Him do so. Then, the ease and rest you'll experience will exceed every fear and anxiety you've ever felt.

**Truth Verses: Matthew 6:31 – 34, Philippians 4:6 – 7,
Isaiah 55:8, Zechariah 4:6 –7**

Beautiful Truth

Day 20

Whatever you prayed to have strength for and deal with, you will be tested on. The enemy will throw everything he can at you to get you to lose your patience and cool about it. Today, keep it together. You're bigger than that. You're stronger than that. You know the tricks of Satan. You can see them coming. When you see your patience and attitude being stretched, ask God for strength and peace right there. Don't try to "work" through it on your own. You can't. Your flesh will want to grumble, act unholy, and do all the things you're trying not to do. Resist it by submitting to God immediately. Tell God "I need You, right now at this very moment. Help me to keep my cool and not get out of character". And He will come to your rescue. He will answer and provide to those who call out to Him.

**Truth Verses: James 4:7 – 8, Ephesians 6:10 – 11,
2 Corinthians 2:11, Psalm 34:4**

Beautiful Truth

Day 21

You will be criticized, judged, and evaluated. But you aren't what people say. You're what God says. Today, get familiar with who God says you are. You're wise and wonderful. You're self-controlled and faith-filled. You're strong and mighty. You're full of joy, peace, and love. You're healthy and healed. You're courageous and fearless. When you know who you are, people's words can't stick with you. Sure, their words may hurt. When they say negative things, it will shake you up. That's natural. But you don't have to receive those words. You don't have to accept and believe them. Quit taking what people say about you as truth. It's just an opinion. You know the truth. The truth is in God's word. The truth is in what He whispers and tells you. Start feeding on that. Start keeping that in your mind and spirit. Then the wrong, negative, ungodly opinions will be of no value to you.

Truth Verses: Matthew 5:11 – 12, John 8:32, Mark 1:11

Beautiful Truth

Day 22

It's the small things that will send you over the edge quicker than anything else. Today, ask God for the grace and patience to deal with the little things. God doesn't want anything causing you discomfort and frustration. His goal is for you to walk in peace at all times in all circumstances. That's why He sent Jesus. That's why He left His Holy Spirit. Quit allowing these small feats to get you out of sorts. It's not worth it. You're more than a conqueror. You have the power to stand strong and walk in peace over everything you encounter. Stop accepting the chaos and start asking God for the strength to overcome.

Truth Verses: 2 Corinthians 12:9, Romans 8:37, John 14:16, Psalm 28:7

Beautiful Truth

Day 23

You can spend your whole life hating someone only to learn you've been hurting no one but yourself. Today, let the bitterness and anger go. Why are you even still mad and upset? Too many times you hold on to things that happened in the past and that's what keeps you stuck right where you are. God can't move you forward when you're glued to the past. He can't bring you peace when you still have anger. He can't help you see His love when hate blinds you. Let it go. Is it easy? Absolutely not. It's a challenge. Your flesh doesn't want to forgive that person. Your mind doesn't want to forget that situation. But the more you hold on to the offense, the further you get away from your future and from the blessings God has for you. Releasing the hurt and pain isn't about appeasing the other person. It's about helping and growing you. When you don't forgive and let things go, you allow people to get the best of you. You allow them to keep you hostage where you are. God doesn't want that. He wants His best for your life. Allow Him to do so. Ask Him to give you the strength and healing you need to forgive and move on. Release the offense to Him. No, your hurt feelings won't go away overnight. But little by little you'll begin to experience and see God's peace and wholeness come alive in your life.

**Truth Verses: Ephesians 4:31 – 32, Isaiah 43:18,
Matthew 6:14, Matthew 18:21 – 22**

Beautiful Truth

Day 24

When it's time, it's time. You can't rush it. You'll just know. Today, you can't force the change you want to see. Too many times you think you're ready when you're honestly not. That's why things haven't come together smoothly. That's why it feels like such an uphill battle. You're pulling against something that isn't ready yet. God's timing is perfect. He doesn't miss a beat or step. Everything He plans for your life is strategic. It's purposeful and for a reason. It's connected. And because it's connected, not getting ahead of Him is important. Sure, you want things to be different right now. Yes, you're looking around seeing change happen for everyone else and you feel like it's not happening for you. But it's not your time yet. It's that simple. God hasn't forgotten about you. Nor have you done anything wrong. God is just still developing and preparing you for what's next. You may think you're ready for it now. But are you? Are you truly prepared for the transition? Are you prepared to deal with new obstacles, new challenges and new people? Can the character you have right now take and keep you where God is planning for you to go? Just because God moves you into a different season in your life doesn't mean it's going to be a walk in the park. It's not going to be easy. It will have its peaks and valleys. Let Him prepare you for that. The things of God aren't going anywhere. What He has for you is for you. It has your name on it. You don't have to beat some time clock. Your turn is coming sooner than you think. Just wait for it.

**Truth Verses: Ecclesiastes 3:1, Psalm 27: 13 – 14,
Proverbs 16:9, Psalm 32:8**

Beautiful Truth

Day 25

God is your protection. He's the one keeping you from harm. He's the one keeping you from the attacks and plans of the enemy. He's the one who brought you favor, not anyone or anything else. Today, quit putting your trust in people and systems. Put your confidence in the Lord. These worldly systems will always let you down when you put your faith in them and not God. The money in your bank account can't protect you. Your fancy title can't keep you. Who and what you know can't save you. God is the one. He's the reason why you haven't fell. He's the reason why your needs have been met. He's the reason why what the enemy planned for evil ultimately turned out for your good. Stop thinking it was because who you are, what you do, or what you have. Everything you have is from God and it belongs to Him. He blessed you with it. And because He blessed you with it, He's going to provide for you in it. He's not going to let you be in lack. He's not letting danger come your way. But your faith must remain in Him. You can't waver and doubt. He is your ultimate source. Quit worrying about the government, the economy, and the affairs of this world. God's got you. He promised to protect the righteous. And you're righteous. You're in this world, but not of it. Remember that.

Truth Verses: Psalm 20:7, Psalm 39:7, Psalm 62:5, John 1:3, Psalm 37:25

Beautiful Truth

Day 26

You have too much to live for to stay stuck in your past. Today, leave the past behind you. Whether good or bad, too many times you get trapped in a memory. You get stuck in how good or bad you felt. You get stuck in how great or horrible a person was to you. You get stuck in "back then." But God is never concerned about "then." He's concerned about now, the present moment. He's concerned about whether you're focused on what's going on in your life today. He's in your right now. He's in this very second and minute. He's blessing you as you are today, not as you were five, 10 or even 20 years ago. Stop focusing your attention on the people and events of the past. God removed those people from your life for a reason. If they were meant to stay, He never would've delivered you from them. But they weren't and you know that. Focus your thoughts on this day for this is the day He has made. He doesn't want you worrying about yesterday and what you've lost. God is a restorer. Whatever you feel was taken from you, tell God about it. He's going to make sure you receive double for your trouble. He's going to make sure your latter is greater and more blessed than your beginning. But you must have faith that what you're gaining is better and far greater than what you're letting go of.

Truth Verses: Isaiah 43:18, Psalm 118:24, Joel 2:25, Isaiah 61:7

Beautiful Truth

Day 27

And if you honestly have nothing to say, say nothing at all. Today, follow the Holy Spirit. Too many times you think you must have a response to what someone is saying. You think if someone comes to you with a problem, you need to be the solution or have all the answers. You think you need to give them your advice. But the truth is you don't. You don't need to do anything, but follow the prompting of the Holy Spirit. And if the Holy Spirit isn't leading you to speak or isn't giving you something to say, why are you trying to force it? Why are you trying to come up with words to lead and direct someone, but God isn't anointing you to do so? Stop it. Quit saying things "just because." Instead, wait on God to lead you in your conversations. The Bible says the words of your mouth and the meditation of your heart need to be pleasing in His sight. But are they pleasing when you're speaking, but not thinking about what you're saying? Are they pleasing when you haven't asked Him to lead you in what to say? God wants to be a part of everything you do, including your conversations. When Jesus spoke, He spoke in love. He uplifted and corrected in love. He encouraged and persuaded in love. Follow His lead. Learn how to die to your flesh and walk in the spirit. Learn how to live in the light of God's presence. Ask Him to help you remain silent today until He moves you into speaking. Take your pride and ego out of it. God wants you to be humble and to honor Him, even in how you speak to others.

Truth Verses: Psalm 19:14, Luke 12:12,
1 Corinthians 16:14, Proverbs 18:21

Beautiful Truth

Day 28

The truth is God will either take care of it or tell you how to handle it. Either way, it's going to be taken care of. Today, that's all you need to know. Stop worrying and wondering about the details. Quit trying to figure out if "this" means "that". Worrying is not what you were created for. You were created to trust God and let Him handle your troubles. The only thing you're supposed to be concerned about is pleasing, honoring, and following Him. But too many times you want the control instead of the obedience. You want to lead instead of follow. Stop it. You have a Father who loves you. Don't you know that if you could truly run your own life God would let you? Don't you know that if He seriously thought you could handle all the things that came your way He would've given you the control? But God knows better than that. He knows there are some things you truly cannot see. And because of that, He's asked you to listen to Him. He's asked you to let Him guide you. Do just that. Stop meditating on things you have no control over. You've prayed about them and God has heard you. Believe that you have received and that it's taken care of. Don't dwell on it. Go enjoy your life and the blessings of God. That's what He's called you to do.

Truth Verses: Luke 12:24 – 31, Colossians 3:2,
Mark 11:24, Ecclesiastes 3:22

Beautiful Truth

Day 29

You don't have all the answers. That's why God appointed other people to help you. Today, stop thinking you're the end all be all. You're not. You don't need to have the answer to every problem. You don't have to know all the time what to do in a crisis. Let other people help you. Do you think God has them around you for nothing? Do you think they are there just for you to order them about? They're not. They are just as smart as you. God has blessed them to be just as wise and talented as you. You're a team. But God also knows where your weaknesses lie. And He knows who to send to compliment those weaknesses. But you have to be open to His help. You have to be receptive to the people He's put in your path to make you better. Don't shut down the blessings and opportunities He's giving you through other people. These people are God-given. They bring value. They challenge you and make you think. They are His blessings, not burdens. They aren't there to be against you, but to be for you. God assigned them to help you be the salt and light of this earth. You need them. Open your eyes. Stop cutting off your help. When you do, you're only hurting yourself and the possibilities God is trying to bring to you. Remember that.

**Truth Verses: 1 Corinthians 12:14 – 20,
Ecclesiastes 4:12, Matthew 5:13 – 16**

Beautiful Truth

Day 30

And why would you serve a God that has you broke, busted, and disgusted? Why would you trust a Father that keeps you in pain? Does that make any sense? It doesn't. Today, God is not the one keeping you down and out. He is not the one keeping you hurt, in pain, sick, confused and unhappy. It's your belief that has you like this. It's the lies and tricks of the enemy you've accepted that have you like this. The enemy wants you to believe God is bad and is causing havoc in your life. He wants you to believe this so that you can stop praying and believing in Him. Why? Because when you stop praying, you have no power. Your words aren't effective. When you don't fellowship with God, you have no authority. When you're mad at Jesus and don't speak His name, demons can't flee. The devil can rule and reign in your life when you have the wrong mindset about Jesus. It's a setup. Stop falling for it. Get your mind renewed about who God is. God is your Father and Jesus is your Savior. He died so that you may live. He was beaten and bruised so that you don't have to hurt in any area of your life. He made the ultimate sacrifice so that you don't have to. Quit thinking God is out to "get" or torture you. God loves you so much. He only wants His very best for you. Go to Him today. Receive His love and abundance. Receive the many blessings and good things He wants to give you. You don't have to put up with anything less than His best in your life. You're just choosing to. Remember that.

Truth Verses: Romans 12:2, James 5:16, John 10:10, Jeremiah 31:3

Beautiful Truth

Day 31

"Strong" doesn't mean never becoming bothered or frustrated. It doesn't mean not crying or feeling like you want to throw in the towel. "Strong" means able to withstand. It means through all the challenges, and the back and forth, you're still here. You're still standing. Today, judge your strength by your position after the storm, not by your behavior through it. Too many times you think God is disappointed in you because you had a bad attitude or felt like giving up. Sure, God doesn't want you feeling or acting this way. But He knows you're not perfect. He knows some things will shake you and rock your world a bit. But are you going to let these things destroy you? Are you going to let them take you out? Are you going to let them turn you bitter and cold, or cause you to give up? Those are the things God is concerned about. A righteous man may fall seven times, but he gets back up again. That's what real strength is. That's how it's measured: by how many times you get back up. Quit looking to go through life's challenges unbothered, or without emotion or feeling. It's not likely to happen. And when you do fall, know that you're righteous, that you're God's beloved. And because of that, you will stand tall again. You will have the victory.

**Truth Verses: Galatians 6:9, Matthew 24:13,
Hebrews 4:15, Proverbs 24:16**

Beautiful Truth

Day 32

Today, maybe the best vengeance you can ever have is to live your life and move on. So many times you want the ones who hurt you to pay for it. You want them to feel the pain you felt. You want their heart to ache. But perhaps that's not the way it's going to happen. Yes, it would make you feel better for the moment. You would even feel justified. But what does it change? Nothing. They still did what they did. They still mistreated you. The outcome is still the outcome. Making them hurt won't change the result. The best thing you could ever do is to forgive yourself, forgive them, and move on. Forgiving them releases their control over you. It lets them know they no longer have power over you. It shows them you've walked away and have separated yourself from the incident, from them, and the past. Let go of these people and past events. You've been holding on to the misery and pain for too long. You've been rehearsing the same incident again and again in your head for years. It's over. God brought you through it. He delivered you. That's your vengeance - that you made it out. You could still be in that same situation with that same person, but you're not. What the enemy meant for bad God used for good. You don't need to punish anyone. Just walk free. Just walk in God's peace and blessings. And He will deal with the appropriate people in His own way in His own time.

**Truth Verses: Matthew 5:7, Genesis 50:20,
Romans 12:19, Proverbs 20:22**

Day 33

Starting over is never easy. But when God gives you a fresh start, you take it. Today, this is your new path. Walk in it. Yes, it feels different and unfamiliar. No, you didn't plan to be at this place. But God did. This is where He wanted and needed you to be. This is what He planned for your life even before you were born. He didn't make a mistake. He knows what He's doing. But His actions won't always make sense to you. Why? Because God works in secret. He doesn't need to tell you everything. He works in the spirit to bring forth the best result for you in the natural. He works behind the scenes, overtime, to bring you to your destiny. And contrary to your belief, this is what's best for you. God sees past what you see right now. He sees past your current feelings. And though He cares about how you feel, it's not going to stop Him from doing what's best in your life. It's not going to stop Him from moving you into new places and environments that will grow and make you better. Your life is not your own. It's God's. When you committed to walking with Him, you gave up your life. You gave up your feelings, emotions, and what you want. That's what walking in God's will is. It's no longer about you, but Him. And if He's told you this is way, then this is the way. There are no "ifs, ands or buts." It's only "yes and amen". It's only "I trust you, Lord." Lean not to your own understanding.

Truth Verses: Jeremiah 1:5, Psalm 18:30, Luke 22:42, 2 Corinthians 1:20, Proverbs 3:5 − 6

Beautiful Truth

Day 34

Ignorance is bliss. Don't open yourself up to what you can't truly handle. Today, what you don't know can't hurt you. Yes, some things are important to know. Sure, you need to be informed. But if being informed causes you to worry, doubt and waver, how important is it? Is it worth your peace, joy, and faith in God? Too many times you open ourselves up to the wrong information. You're listening to the news and the media. Then, you wonder why you feel bad. You wonder why you can't feel the presence of God or hear from Him. You wonder why you feel depressed, fearful, jealous, bitter and angry. You can't experience the presence of God when you're feeding on that type of information all day. You can't feel like God has your back and you're protected if you're watching and listening to what's going on in this world. It's messing with your mind. Shut it off. It's a trick of the enemy. He uses the media and airwaves to pull you in and to keep you in fear. He gives you access into the lives of other people and creates jealousy to keep you feeling bad about your own life, to make you think you're not doing enough or that you're missing out. But you're not. Quit opening yourself up to these same tricks. If something makes you feel bad, worried, panicked, or fearful, stop listening to it. Turn off the TV and tune into the word of God. Turn off the depressing songs and put His words in your ear. Stop searching through people's social media profiles and search His word. You'll never get to where God needs you to be doing the same old thing. Yes, God has great and better things in store for you. But you don't get it by feeding on the things of this world. You're in this world, but not of it. You're separated and called out. Act like it.

Truth Verses: Proverbs 4:23, 1 Peter 5:8, John 15:19, Psalm 1:2

Beautiful Truth

34

Day 35

And just because it's shiny and brand new doesn't mean it's without flaws. No matter how great something is in your life it's going to take some time to get used to it. Today, give yourself room to adjust. Change is not always easy. Nor it is always pleasant. But in God, it's worthwhile. Too many times you make assumptions and judgments about an entire situation when it's too early to tell whether it's good or bad. You're just getting started, but because it feels different, you think it's automatically wrong. But it's not. Different doesn't equal wrong. It's just not what you're used to. And even though you're not used to it, it doesn't mean it's bad for you. Nor does it mean it's perfect. Nothing in this world is perfect except Jesus. He is the perfect one. Everything else in this world comes with flaws and something you'll have to adjust to or deal with. From people to possessions, start being mindful of that. Stop thinking every time you encounter something new it's going to be without challenge or imperfection. Set realistic expectations for the new blessings God brings into your life. Yes, He provides you with great and wonderful things. But wonderful doesn't mean perfection or easy. Expect the people you encounter to have faults. Expect them to have good and bad days. Expect the situations you come across to be rocky at times. It's called life. It's called learning how to balance. It's called leaning on the arms of the Lord. The ease of doing things and accomplishing goals doesn't come from not having any problems or "bumps" in the road. It comes from knowing how to rely on and look towards God. It comes from knowing He will give you the strength, wisdom and power to overcome any setback you face. Remember that.

Truth Verses: Ecclesiastes 3:1 – 8, John 16:33, 2 Corinthians 4:17

Beautiful Truth

Day 36

Sometimes ignoring the negativity is the best way to win the battle. Today, you don't have to fight fire with fire. Submit your words and thoughts unto the Lord. When someone attacks or comes against you, too many times you want to strike back. You want to lash out. You want to stand up for yourself and make sure people know where you stand. But the truth is most people already know where you stand. They know what they can and cannot bring your way. They know what you will and won't stand for. You don't have to show and tell them who's boss. Your silence speaks volumes way more than your words ever could. How? Your silence shows self-control. It shows you trust your Heavenly Father to fight your battles. It shows you don't need to "flex your muscles," but you trust God to take care of you. You trust Him to deal with the difficult people and situations in your life. You trust Him to lead and guide you on when to speak and when not to. Start living your life this way. Stop being so quick to "set the record straight." God is not looking for you to go into situations like a blazing fire. He's looking for you to let Him in. He's looking for you to seek His help instead of seeking your own. He's looking for you to trust His ways instead of your ways. He's looking to make things work in your favor, even in disputes and difficult situations. Give God the chance to do so. It doesn't matter how big or small the issue is. Bring Him in. Quit looking to fight things all on your own. Cast your care and let God truly take of you.

Truth Verses: Roman 12:21, 2 Chronicles 20:15,
Galatians 5:22, Proverbs 29:11

Day 37

If God is sending someone your way to help and bless you, let them. Today, you're not that busy to receive help. Nor should you be so closed off from the world that you don't allow the love of the Lord and His kindness to shine upon you. So many times you complain about the world and people not being loving enough, but when God provides the opportunity for you to receive love, you shun it. You complain. You feel inconvenienced. You don't want to be bothered. You have too much to do so you shut people out. But God shows His love for you on earth through people and their loving kindness. When people just want to be in your presence and be around you, that means something. It means they are drawn to your light. It means you're being the salt of the earth and walking as Christ walked. Don't stop being the light. Yes, you have many things to do and manage. But slow down. Don't be the "Martha." Be the "Mary." Take a break. Learn how to sit at the feet of Jesus. Soak up His love when He's giving it to you through others. Take the compliments He's dishing out. Bask in the enjoyment of others. Quit looking at people as a burden or bother to you. When your life is full of people and relationships, it's a blessing. That's truly what walking in the prosperity and abundance of the Lord is. It's about all aspects of your life, including the love and riches God has provided for you through other people.

Truth Verses: 1 John 4:7 – 8, John 8:12, Mark 9:50,
Luke 10: 38 – 42

Beautiful Truth

Day 38

And where you're going is so much better than where you are right now. God has so much more in store for you. Today, this isn't the end. God has more to show you and more for you to bring to the table. Quit getting caught up in your "right now." It doesn't matter how old you are. It doesn't matter what you have or haven't done. It doesn't matter how many mistakes you've made. Are you living for God? Are you living for His will? Do you desire what He has for you? Then, you can still be used by Him, even with the mess you think you've made of your life. Contrary to your belief, God isn't looking at your messes. You are. You're the one believing the lies of the enemy. Stop listening to him. God can still get something out of your life. He can and will place you where you need to be. He can and will make you successful. That's His promise to you. That's your seal for the future. Stop thinking where you are right now is all there is. It isn't. Get excited about your future. Get excited about your life. Yes, it's hard to see through the maze and the drama right now. Sure, there's been hurt and pain. But have hope in the Lord. Greater is on the other side. It's already written and accounted for.

Truth Verses: Job 8:7, John 8:44, Hebrews 6: 18 – 19, Luke 8:22

Beautiful Truth

Day 39

Just because you're happy about what's going on in your life doesn't mean everyone else will be. Some people will just not celebrate you. Today, learn to celebrate yourself. Contrary to your belief, you're not living for the approval of others. You're not living for their applause, acceptance, or to make them feel good. You're living for God. He is your number one priority. He is your number one fan. And if God is in your corner, if God is telling you He's proud, and this is the way He wants you to lead your life, why are you even entertaining what someone else is saying? Why are they even getting your time, attention, or ear? Yes, you love others and value their opinions. But at the end of the day, this is your life. God created and birthed you on this earth for such a time as this. You only get one shot. You only get one chance at this thing called life. Yes, God restores and gives you second chances. But only once are you born. Only once do you have the chance to live, breathe and do God's will. Do it the way He's instructing you to. Quit being concerned that you don't have anyone backing or cheering for you. Did people always cheer for Jesus? Did He always get to do the thing that pleased others and made them happy? No. Everything Jesus did was contrary and combative to what the world said, but it was pleasing to God. Take a page from His book. Follow His life. Stop being so desperate to have others support you. God will bring the right people into your life that will do exactly what you need. Plus, He'll be there for you. He'll never leave you nor forsake you. Remember that.

**Truth Verses: Romans 8:31, Mark 6:1 −4,
Deuteronomy 31:6, Deuteronomy 5:33**

Beautiful Truth

Day 40

And sometimes you just have to do what you have to do. Today, quit feeling guilty about these life decisions you've had to make. Was it good for you? Did it truly bring hurt or harm to your life? No. Then, what's the problem? Making hard decisions are a part of life. God never said it would be easy or pleasant. Nor did He say you would enjoy making every decision you'd have to face. You won't. Some stuff is just hard. Some stuff just requires your obedience over sacrifice. Some stuff just requires your blood, sweat, and tears. And no, you won't always understand it. No, you won't always feel good about it. But some decisions that you feel bad about now will bless you later. Recognize that. God is not out to make you feel good all the time. He's not looking to keep your emotions satisfied. He's looking to do what's best for you. And when He leads you to make certain decisions, it's for a reason. It's for your good in the long run. Learn how to trust God over your own logic and reasoning. Trust Him over your emotions or feelings. If you made the best decision you could, it's ok. Stop worrying and wondering about it. Stop feeling guilty and condemned. It's over and done. The rest is for God to work out.

Truth Verses: 1 Samuel 15:22, Psalm 118:8, Proverbs 28:26

Beautiful Truth

Day 41

And nothing is ever as bad as it seems in your mind. Today, don't let the enemy deceive you. Yes, it's not the best situation. But you are still standing. You are still here. You are still living and breathing, here to see and fight another day. Let that count for something. Let that minister to your heart and mind. God isn't finished with you yet. This season and time of uncertainty and confusion is just a period in your life. The enemy wants you to see this season as more than that. He wants you to view it as life-changing and life-altering, like you're never coming out of it. But the devil is a liar. You are coming out. And you're coming out better and greater than you were before. You're coming out stronger and wiser. You're coming out full of power and might. Your life isn't over. That's the enemy putting those thoughts in your head. That's him using these scare tactics to intimidate you. But that's all they are - tactics. The enemy has no power over you. He is all bark, but no bite. Why? Because he's already defeated. You hold the power and the authority. It's in your mouth. It's in your words. It's in your attitude. It's in your belief and faith. You can't afford to keep forgetting that. Yes, it feels "strange" calling those things that be not as they are and to speak to your mountains. But do you want them removed? Do you want to keep getting the same result you're getting? No. Then, fight the good fight. Gird up your mind with the things of God. Speak His word and His goodness. Life comes with ups and downs. But the darkness the enemy is trying to place in your mind is never God's will for you. Remember that.

**Truth Verses: Matthew 21:21, Romans 4:17,
1 Timothy 6:12, 1 Peter 1:13 (KJV)**

Beautiful Truth

Day 42

Honestly, it shouldn't matter what anyone else is doing. What did God tell you to do? Today, follow God's instructions for your own life. Quit being so engrossed with everyone else's business. Being concerned with what someone else is doing shows you really don't enjoy or care too much about your own life. People who are at peace and have joy in their life don't have time to be worried about other people. They're too concerned with the things of God. They're too busy carrying out the work of their Heavenly Father. They don't have the time or energy to waste being distracted on the wrong thing. They know it only brings delayed progress in their own life. Learn how to be one of those people. Just because you don't like what God is calling you to do right now doesn't mean you need to meddle in someone else's affairs. Pay attention to your own business. Get busy with what God assigned you to do. What has He told you to do that you're still putting off? Who has He told you to help that you keep ignoring? What goals has He told you to set, but you haven't completed? You have enough you need to focus on. You have no time to wonder, criticize, or complain about what others are doing. Get focused on you. God loves you. He wants you to progress just like He wants the next person to progress. But you can't be so preoccupied with their life that you neglect your own. It's called prioritizing. Remember that.

Truth Verses: 1 Thessalonians 4:11, Proverbs 31:27, Psalm 37:3

Beautiful Truth

Day 43

You're so used to bad you don't even realize when you have it good. Today, this is a good thing. What God is doing right now in your life is a blessing. It's His hand working in your life. It's Him having your back. Can't you see it? Can't you see how wonderful it is? Or are you still blinded by the bad experiences you've had? Stop it. God didn't bring you out of your circumstances to paralyze you. He brought you out so you could learn from them, so you could use those experiences to help others and yourself go forward. Quit allowing these past events to hold you back. Yes, it was bad. But there's better on the other side of it. This isn't the end. Your life isn't over. God is a restorer. For every bad situation you've been through, there's better to come. Your latter is greater and more blessed than your beginning. Change your mindset and perception about what God is doing in your life right now. Change how you're seeing it. There's more good around you than evil. There's more working for you than against you. But you must be open to it. You must open your eyes to see it.

Truth Verses: James 1:17, Psalm 107:6, Joel 2:25 – 26, Ephesians 1:18

Beautiful Truth

Day 44

And you're the righteousness of God in Christ. You're not waiting on God to bless you. Whatever God sends your way is blessed because you're in it. Today, know who you are. You don't have to sit around panicked, waiting for the miracle to happen. You don't have to be nervous or scared thinking good things won't come to you. They will. God is on your side. He is in your court. He has provided grace and favor every step of the way. The blessing is not the car, house, promotion, or any other material thing you're asking for or waiting on. Every day you rise you're blessed. You're blessed coming in and going out. You're blessed on your good days and your bad. You're blessed when you're right and when you're wrong. You're blessed when you're happy and when you're sad. It never changes. Your stance in the kingdom of God is continual because God is with you. And the things He provides for you are a result of His blessing and goodness. Quit thinking you must beg, borrow, or prove yourself to receive things from the Lord. You are a child of God. Blessings come with your name on them. Why? Because God is in you and you're in Him. You don't have to be anxious. The "blessing" is not the one that's blessed. You are. The blessing finds you, not the other way around. Stop chasing after things, hoping and praying they can be yours or they will come to you. You're favored. Everything you touch prospers. You can have whatever you say you can have. You hold the power. Goodness and mercy follows you all the days of your life. Remember that.

Truth Verses: 2 Corinthians 5:21, Deuteronomy 28:6, Genesis 39:2, Deuteronomy 30:9

Beautiful Truth

Day 45

God will supply, not some, not a little, but all your needs according to His riches and glory. Today, believe that. Quit worrying about what you want and if you'll get it. Do you need it? Is it essential? Is it going to make you better and enhance your life? Then, you'll get it. God's going to supply it. It's that simple. He hasn't forgotten about you. He hasn't forgotten your prayers, the very words you've spoken to Him. He hasn't forgotten what you desire. He knows. And if this thing you desire isn't going to hurt you, God will provide it. But He's not obligated to give you anything you want. Why? Because what you want could hurt you. What you want could be the very thing to destroy you. And God will never do anything to hurt or harm you. He isn't trying to lead you somewhere you'll regret later. He loves you and only wants what's best for you. You can trust Him for that. You can have faith and believe Him for that. Stop putting all your woes and worries into getting the things you want. Trust that God knows you well enough to supply what you need, the very things that will sustain and keep you each and every day.

Truth Verses: Philippians 4:19, Jeremiah 29:11, Psalm 55:22, Isaiah 46:4

Beautiful Truth

Day 46

Sometimes the best thing for you to do is the hardest thing to do. But you must face it. Today, push through what's hard to get to what's better. The difficulty of the matter isn't what's important. That's not what this challenge is about. You're focused on the wrong thing. What this is about is getting to the other side, to the next thing God has for you. Stop holding up your own progress because you're looking at how hard something is. Life is challenging. You'll have to make difficult decisions at times. But that's a part of life. That's what you signed up for when you became an adult. God never promised you ease and comfort every day. Some days the walk will be long and hard. Some days you'll feel like you're on your last leg. But you don't duck and hide, or avoid doing what's right because it's hard. You don't stay stagnant or get complacent because what's ahead looks too difficult. As hard as it may be, nothing is too difficult for God. He is with you. There's nothing you're going through or will go through that He can't fix or give you the grace to bear. He's your Father. He's not going to let you fall. Trust in Him during this time. If God is bringing you to it, He has a plan to get you through it. You're going to make it. You're going to prevail. Just wait and see.

Truth Verses: 2 Corinthians 4:8, Matthew 7: 13 – 14, Jeremiah 32:27, Psalm 37:24

Beautiful Truth

Day 47

If you're unhappy, do something about it. The power is not in someone else's hand. It's in yours. Today, quit looking to other people to make you happy. This is why you're always disappointed. This is why you and God can't get anywhere. You're so busy praying to Him about how to change someone else that you don't give Him enough time to deal with you. "They" are not the problem. You are. You are God's concern. Sure, He cares about everyone. But when you're coming to Him, His attention is on you. He is concerned about you and why you're not happy. He's concerned with why you're displeased with life, why you don't seem to be content. And the truth is you're not satisfied with life because you're putting all your eggs in the wrong basket. You've put your heart and faith in people, not in God. People are fickle. They change with the wind. Yes, some are reliable and dependable. But every day you rise your faith shouldn't be in them. It should be in God. God is your constant and never changing. He's not going to love you one minute and hate you the next. He's not fickle. God isn't trying to control you or make you his puppet. All God wants is you. All He wants is for you to trust and rely on Him. As hard as it is, learn how to do just that. Quit looking to someone else to see what's going on or to make you feel good about yourself. Look to God. Tell Him what's going on in your life. Tell Him your feelings, fears, and disappointments. Then, let Him pour His love on you. Let Him be faithful and dependable to you. Once you get a taste of relying on Jesus, you won't be so quick to run to anyone else.

**Truth Verses: Psalm 146:3, Jeremiah 17:5,
Numbers 23:19, 1 Corinthians 8:6**

Beautiful Truth

Day 48

Some people are just difficult to deal with. But that doesn't mean you stop dealing with them. You don't give up and run away from them. Today, love people where they are. That's all God has called you to do. He hasn't called you to change, criticize or judge them. It's not your place to tell them what they're doing wrong. God is the one who transforms and changes. He is the one who convicts and disciplines, not you. Quit thinking you must be the one to show people what they need to do with their life. This is why you're stressed out and are not progressing. Your focus is on the wrong thing. God has called you to be focused on you and the changes He's telling you to make. Your focus isn't to get others in line or on your path. You're not their ruler. Yes, it's good to help others and to be there for them. But what they do and why they're doing it isn't your battle. Let God handle it. Let Him deal with your loved ones, family and friends. Your critical attitude isn't helping them. Take a step back. Ask God to give you the strength to love and accept them just as they are. Wouldn't you want the same done for you?

**Truth Verses: John 13:34, James 4:12, Matthew 7:1,
1 Corinthians 3:6 – 9**

Beautiful Truth

Day 49

It doesn't matter how many people tell you your life is good. If you don't see it as good, you'll always think you're beneath. You'll always think you're missing out or God has given you the short end of the stick. Today, it's your perception that's the problem. Why do you see things the way you see them? Why are you constantly looking for the bad? Examine that. Seeing everything as bad and a struggle is not of God. Sure, some situations you've gone through in life haven't been the best. Yes, they've been difficult to handle. But they don't define you. They don't shape you. That's not who you are. That's not how every situation will turn out. The enemy wants you to think from now on this is what you'll get. He wants you to speak and believe that "bad" or "challenging" is all that's out there. If he can get you to believe that, he'll get you to speak that. Why? Because that's where your power lies. It's your words that create and transform situations. Stop allowing these negative thoughts to push you into speaking negative things. God is good. You know that. He's above every tragedy you've experienced. He's above every hurt and pain you've felt. He's bigger than the deception you faced and greater than what you lost. Put that thought in your head. Speak that. Speak His goodness. Yes, it's hard when what you see doesn't line up to what you're speaking. But kill your emotions. The spirit of Christ in you is bigger than how you feel or what the enemy is telling you. Remember that.

Truth Verses: Proverbs 6:2, Psalm 118:1, Galatians 5:24, 1 John 4:4

Beautiful Truth

Day 50

Don't let fear get in the way of what you know you're supposed to be doing. Don't let the enemy win over you like that. Today, go forth, even if you're afraid. Too many times you take fear as a sign you're doing something wrong or that you shouldn't be doing it at all. But that's not true. You know what you're supposed to be doing. You know what God has called you to. You feel it in your heart. You sense it deep in your soul. The fear, panic, and worry is only a distraction. It's the only thing the enemy can use to get you off the path, make you question what you're doing and doubt God. Don't fall for it. God hasn't given you a spirit of fear. Nor would He tell you to do anything that would put you in harm's way. You know your Father. Hold on to what you know about Him. Trust in that. That's how you combat the fear you're feeling. That's how you shut it down. You shut it down with your confidence in your Lord. And if He says this is the way, follow it. Quit questioning and analyzing it. You don't have to be fearful when your God is with you. You don't have to be scared when He's covering you. He is your almighty Savior. He has all power and authority. Learn to rely on Him. He's the only one that's going to get you through this. Remember that.

Truth Verses: 2 Timothy 1:7, Proverbs 3:26, Isaiah 30:21

Beautiful Truth

Day 51

You're so worried and focused on what was that you can't see the blessing in what is. Today, open your eyes. God isn't in the "yesterdays". He's in the now, in what's present. He's right here in this very moment. And every time you go back and look at what's behind, you slap Him in the face. How? Because you're not seeing and appreciating what God is blessing you with right now. He hasn't provided His blessings for you to whine and complain about them. He hasn't blessed you so you can say what's missing and how it's not like it used to be. It's not going to be like it was. This is new and different. But just because it's new doesn't mean it's not good for you. It doesn't mean things are going downhill. Stop letting the enemy tell you that. He wants you to think that anything new in your life is wrong so that you never move forward and stay right where you are in the same situation getting the same results. Don't fall for it. God is about progress and forward movement. He's always looking to elevate you. No, things aren't going to be the same and you'll have to adjust. But you're ready for this. You can handle it. God graced you where you were and He's giving you grace now. He's giving you the wisdom, favor, and revelation you need to be successful. Trust Him in this place. Trust where He's leading you. He's never steered you wrong or made a mistake. You don't have to hold on to the past. Walk into this new season with God and with confidence.

Truth Verses: Philippians 1:6, Psalm 62:8, 2 Corinthians 12:9

Beautiful Truth

Day 52

This is not just a test. It's a testimony. Today, go through this trial and period in your life. Yes, it's difficult and challenging. But it's a part of your story. It's a part of what God wants you to share. It's how you're going to help other people and spread His word. You can't be a fighter without a fight. You can't be a hero without a battle. It doesn't work like that. If God already declared you victorious, you know there's going to be a battle. You know there's going to be something you must face and overcome. Get your mind prepared for it. Quit thinking you can breeze through life and have victory. Quit being shocked by these trials and tests. Life is not perfect. God hasn't promised you the easiest, most convenient way out all the time. What He did promise is that He would use you, that your heartache and struggle won't be in vain. Every tear you shed, you will restore in joy. You will receive double for your trouble. God isn't allowing you to go through the storm and rain without receiving the promise later. Your miracle is here. Your promise is here. But you get to it through this challenge. You get to it through this process. Remember that.

Truth Verses: 1 Peter 4:12 –13, 2 Samuel 22:30, Isaiah 61:7, Isaiah 43:2

Beautiful Truth

Day 53

But you made it. You can talk about how bad it was all you want. But the truth is you stood the test. You took every dart the enemy threw and still overcame. You still had the victory. You still came out walking tall and strong. Today, pat yourself on the back. Take a bow. You've overcome and outlasted a lot. You've been through the wilderness and the storm. You've been through the hardest times of your life. But you're still here. The enemy didn't defeat or destroy you. Every weapon he formed didn't prosper. Every attack he planned failed. He tried, but he couldn't touch you. He couldn't stop the plan of God. He couldn't stop the blessings, the favor, the goodness God has on your life. You're still standing for a reason and a purpose. Be thankful for that. Praise God for that. Too many times you go through life's challenges, battling so much, jumping from one fight to the next, but you never acknowledge or see how far you've come. You never take a moment to look at all God has brought you through and how He's kept you. Take the time to see the growth you've had. Take the time to see the progress you've made. Take the time to see how much you've truly had to endure and fight to get to where you are. This was no easy feat. This wasn't a battle everyone could've won. But God. But His grace and hand is upon you. It's sufficient for you. It's been everything and all you needed to make it through.

Truth Verses: Psalm 91:7, John 10:28 – 29, Psalm 27:13, 2 Corinthians 9:8

Beautiful Truth

Day 54

And maybe you did spend too much time staying in what you knew was a bad situation. But God isn't punishing you for that. He still wants to deliver you. Today, God is coming to your rescue. It doesn't matter how long you've been in the situation or how terrible it is. It doesn't matter if you did right or wrong. God is a deliverer. He wants to bring you out. He wants you out of this circumstance and the next one. Why? Because He loves you. Just because other people have left you high and dry doesn't mean God will. He isn't like that. Yes, you have free will and it's your decision whether or not you want to stay in an unpleasant situation or keep trying. But the minute you decide you need the Lord, He's there. He's not leaving or turning His back on you. Whether it's to change the situation or remove you from it, the second you called, God answered. Stop thinking it's your fault that the situation you're in has lasted so long. Yes, you've made mistakes. But none of that has anything to do with God's faithfulness to you. He's always looking to rescue you. Give the situation over to God. Only He has the power to change and set free. Stop thinking "What am I going to do?" Turn to God and watch Him do the very thing you need.

Truth Verses: Psalm 18:6, Psalm 91:14 – 15, Psalm 144:2, James 4:10

Beautiful Truth

Day 55

If you believe the lie of the enemy that you've been dealt a bad hand in life, then that's how you'll always see it. You'll always have the wrong perspective about your life and everything in it. Today, you haven't come up short in your life. Nor has God given you a raw deal. Nothing is missing or lacking. You have received everything you need. The truth is you not receiving the very thing you wanted is a blessing. It's actually God's saving grace and hand upon you. You think you've lost, but you've really won. Just because the enemy is trying to show you everything you're missing doesn't mean you'd be better off with it. If you really needed it, you'd have it, right? God would've allowed it in your life. He would've allowed that situation to come forth. But He didn't. Why? Because He knows something you don't. What you wanted is not the best for you and God has something better. Your job is not to pout about what you didn't receive. It's to get to God's plan and assignment for your life. Your waiting has not been in vain. God has not forgotten you. He is still coming through - just not in the way you thought. Just not in the situation you thought. Just not with the person you thought. Let your pretenses go. He has something different in mind. Stop thinking so negatively and short-sided about the situation. It is all for your good and benefit, to bring out the best God has in store for you.

Truth Verses: James 1:4, Isaiah 55:8, Isaiah 49:4, Psalm 119:71

Beautiful Truth

Day 56

Everybody has a breaking point. What's yours? Today, know your limits. As much as you want to be, you're not superman. You cannot do everything and be everything to everyone without burning out. Nobody is that strong. Nobody is that awesome, great or wonderful. Everyone has a point where they will tip over and fall apart. Quit making yourself believe that you don't. The enemy is deceiving you, calling what you're doing "strength" so that you can wear out and wear down. He's making you think it's ok because people need you. Yes, you are called to be a blessing. But when did God say to neglect yourself in the process? When did He say it was acceptable to run yourself ragged? He didn't. God wants you at your best always. That's why He sent His son Jesus so that you may live abundantly. Jesus didn't die so that you could be broke down, busted and disgusted. How does that display God's glory or His will for your life? Get yourself together. Stop letting people pull your strings like a puppet. Learn how to set boundaries and say no. You cannot continue to do everything you're doing in the name of the Lord. That's not truth. The Lord knows how to rest and to be purposeful with His time. Follow His lead. Until you do, you'll just keep feeling like you're feeling - frustrated with life.

Truth Verses: John 10:10, Psalm 90:12, 1 Peter 5:8, Genesis 2:2 – 3

Beautiful Truth

Day 57

And when will it be your turn? When God decides it's your turn. It's that hard, but it's that simple. Today, you can't make anything happen in this life. You just have to wait until it's your turn. The truth is your moment in the sun isn't far away. It's closer than what you think. Quit thinking it's never going to happen. It is going to happen. God said it and He promised it. He hasn't forgotten or forsaken you. He's heard your prayers and cries. He's seen your heartache and pain, your long days and hard nights, all the frustration and confusion you've gone through. And He's going to do something about it. But in His perfect timing, not yours. You can't rush this. You can't force the change you want to bring about so badly. Nor can you worry yourself sick about it. The situation is in God's hands. Put it there and leave it there. Give yourself a break. Rest from fretting about what to do, how and when. God is going to line everything up together in your life when the time is just right. Until then, you'll be waiting. No, you're not a bad person. You're the righteousness of God in Christ. And God loves you so much. So much that He will not give you anything that will not turn out for your good. Stop thinking God is trying to make you suffer with this wait. He's not. He's setting you up for a blessing of a lifetime. Remember that.

**Truth Verses: 2 Peter 3:8, Psalm 27:14, Psalm 37:34,
Romans 5:3 — 4**

Beautiful Truth

Day 58

Life is all about what you make it. Sure, you may not have been given every opportunity in the world. But are you going to let that stop you? Are you really going to let that hold you back from all God has promised you? Today, fight for something. You're not supposed to just sit back and take it. It's not "que sera, sera, what will be, will be." You have a say and part in your life. The Lord is with you. He has put His might and strength in you. Everything you have on the inside comes from God. Through Him and in Him you're as strong as you need to be. You're mightier than you think. Quit sitting back and allowing this world to shake you. Pull from that fight inside you. Fight for your kids. Fight for your career. Fight for your marriage. Fight for your household. Fight your community. Fight for your family and friends. Do something. God hasn't blessed you to just "exist." Nor has he created you to wallow in self-pity and feel bad about yourself. No matter what has happened, no matter how horrible and tragic it has been, God is able. With Him on your side, you can get to your promise land. Stop sitting there accepting lack, giving into the negative, drama-filled circumstances in your life. You're more than a conqueror. Get up and act like it.

Truth Verses: Acts 17:28, Ephesians 6:10, Romans 8:37

Beautiful Truth

Day 59

There's nothing perfect in this world. Everything you encounter will have its ups and downs. But you're more than equipped to handle it. Today, you don't need to run away. You don't need to avoid or step back in fear. Nor do you need a perfect scenario to feel good about your life. You were born strong. God created you full of might. The perfect situation has nothing to do with your strength or ability to endure. You can persevere through anything regardless of the situation. Why? Because you're a child of God. You're righteous through Him. Everything you need is already in you. It's a mindset and a knowing. Quit allowing the enemy to tell you differently. Quit allowing him to get in your head and make you believe that if your life isn't "tipping through the tulips" at all times you need to change it or stop doing what you're doing. You don't. Life has its peaks and valleys. But it's through those valleys you grow stronger. It's through those peaks you find and share your testimony. Your story and testimony don't come with perfection or feeling good. They come in the dark days and imperfections. Stop being upset about it. Instead, embrace these hard places in your life. Trust God to bring you through them. Why? Because you've come too far and God's been with you too long for Him to leave you now.

Truth Verses: Haggai 2:4, Psalm 23:4, Matthew 28:20

Beautiful Truth

Day 60

You're not supposed to trust in people and things. You're supposed to trust in God. Today, quit putting your faith in the wrong things. This is why you're worried and anxious. People are faulty. They change with the wind. They are for you one minute and against you the next. They understand you today and are confused by you tomorrow. No matter how hard you try and how hard you work, you can't please them. There will always be something you're doing or not doing that will please or displease them. You know that. So why are you putting all your energies towards them? Why are you working overtime to make them happy? Why are you trusting in their words and in what they're telling you? Why do you believe they know more and can do more for you than God? Stop deceiving yourself. You can have access to every resource in the world and know millions of people, but if you don't know the Lord, you're walking on shaky ground. Learn how to put your faith in God and God alone. He's the one who is unshakable. His words never fail. He never lets you down. Each day you rise believe God is looking out for you. Know deep in your heart that He loves you. Know His character. He's never going to do anything to harm you. Challenges come. You'll experience hurt and pain at times. But it's never God's intention to punish or make you suffer for His pleasure. There's purpose behind every tear you've cried and pain you've felt. God's going to use it for something greater and better. That's why He's worthy of your trust.

Truth Verses: Jeremiah 17:5 – 8, Psalm 62:7 – 8, Romans 8:28

Beautiful Truth

Day 61

You can't look forward while going backward. Either you're moving on or you're not. But you can't do both. Today, when God says it's over, it's over. There is no turning or looking back. There is no "but." He's telling you what to do. He's telling you to walk away and go on. So what are you holding on for? What is it doing for you? What is staying in the past, clinging to what "was" doing for your life? Nothing. All it is doing is keeping you in the same place in the same environment with the same people. God is about growth. He's about steady movement and progression. He takes your life from moment to moment. He moves you little by little to what He has for you. And once that moment is done, it's done. If you were supposed to stay in it, God would've told you. He would've made provision for it. But He didn't. Recognize when it's time to move on. He has something beyond this point for you. But you have to cooperate. Stop holding on to what God is trying to pull away from you. You say you want a change. You keep praying for different. Letting go of this situation, relationship or setup will make your life different. It will bring the freshness you need. But you can't have it both ways. You can't hold on and walk in faith at the same time. Decide: either you're going where God is sending you or you're not.

Truth Verses: 1 Samuel 16:1, Exodus 23:30, John 5:8

Beautiful Truth

Day 62

Either it's going to happen or it's not. It's that simple. Today, there's no use in worrying yourself about this situation. You've been over it in your head a million times. You've tried to figure out how it would turn out. But the truth is you don't know. You don't have any clue how it will really shake out. And that's ok. All you need to know is God is on your side. He's for you, with you and loves you. Because of that, you know it's going to be alright. You know it's going to work out for your good, even if it doesn't turn out the way you wanted. Your way and plans are not God's. His way is the one that will lead you to success, joy, and the most peace. Yes, it's hard and disappointing when you don't receive what you want when you want it. But that's how you feel right now. God is looking at the long-term. He's looking at what will be best for you not only today, but tomorrow, a year from now and even decades from now. He knows how one wrong decision can impact your life and have a ripple effect. Let Him work this situation out for you. Don't fret or worry. God's not going to let anything happen to you. You've asked Him for guidance. You've asked Him to lead you to the right thing, to what He wants and needs you to do. Trust in Him. He will guide and take you exactly where you need to be.

Truth Verses: Deuteronomy 5:33, John 14:1, Psalm 25:5

Beautiful Truth

Day 63

Just because that's how you used to be doesn't mean that's how you are now. You're different. And that's a good thing. Today, enjoy the progress you've made. Too many times you let people remind you of where you've been instead of where you are now and where you're going. God has changed you. He has transformed you from the inside out. He has set you free. You are a new creature in Him. Quit listening to what other people are saying about you. Quit believing who they say you are, allowing their perceptions of you to steal your joy and rob you of your progress. The truth is some people will only see you as you were. They can't get past the child you were and the mistake you made. They can't get past what you said or did. They keep holding on to it. But God doesn't. He's forgiven you. Your mistakes have been washed under the blood and thrown into the sea of forgetfulness. You're as clean as the freshly fallen snow. Walk in it. Don't question it. Don't look to the left or the right. Don't look behind you. Stay focused on where you are. Stay focused on moving forward. God is so very proud of you. He's pleased with you. Be pleased with yourself.

Truth Verses: 2 Corinthians 5:17, 1 Corinthians 13:11, Isaiah 1:18, Joshua 1:7

Beautiful Truth

Day 64

Honestly, it's not your cross to bear. Today, quit feeling responsible for other people's problems. Did you create these problems? Did you get them into the situation? No. Then, why do you feel it's your job to get them out of it? Why do you feel you must be the savior of their situations? Contrary to your belief, you don't need to be their savior. God is their savior. He is the only one that can deliver others. He is the only one that can bring them out. Yes, you feel empathy for what they're experiencing. But don't confuse empathy with responsibility and accountability. They're accountable to this situation, not you. They need to figure this out, not you. Sure, you can help and suggest. But you still have your own life to lead. God is still holding your feet to the fire about your own household, family, job, church, community, and what you've been assigned to. That's your priority. Help all you can, but set better boundaries by staying in your lane. The minute someone else's life starts consuming yours and you're no longer feeling at peace or taking care of your own responsibilities, you're out of balance. You're too involved. Take a step back. Reprioritize and reset your boundaries. Tell others "no" for a change. Tell them you need to figure out your own life and schedule before you commit to anything. Then, and only then can you go back to and remain in peace.

Truth Verses: Galatians 6:5, Romans 14:19, Proverbs 16:9

Beautiful Truth

Day 65

Honestly, you can't worry about what you lost. The truth is you have so much more to gain. Today, quit focusing on what used to be. If that was what you were supposed to have and be doing, and if that was who you were supposed to be doing it with, you would be. It's that plain and simple. God doesn't make a mistake. What's yours is yours. It's final. It doesn't change because of your behavior, attitude or mood. If God has declared something for you, not a demon in hell can stop it. But what He declares not to be yours is a plan you can't touch either. You must trust that this is the right way for you and you must be ok with it. Why? Because whatever or whoever doesn't stay attached to you isn't a part of the plan God has for you on earth. God is about your eternal goodness. What is great in one season He'll remove in the next if it's bringing you down and stopping His purpose. He isn't interested in making you comfortable. He's interested in you fulfilling His purpose on earth. Stop being concerned with what or who has left you. God has bigger and better in store. He doesn't want you to settle, thinking what "was" is all there is to your life. It's not. You're God's righteousness. He's looking to bless you in the present and future. Get to your blessings. Let go of the past. Go forth in the future, to where God's leading you.

Truth Verses: Isaiah 43:18 – 19, Psalm 40:5, Genesis 22:17

Beautiful Truth

Day 66

You have no reason to be envious or to want what someone else has. God hasn't forgotten you. Today, your day is coming. Wait on the Lord. Yes, you've been waiting and believing for a long time now. Sure, you're tired of hoping and praying for the same thing. But did God say to pray until you get weary, then stop? Did He say believe until you're tired? No. God said pray without ceasing. Ask and keep asking. Believe and keep believing. God never promised you a quick and easy anything. He never said victory would come immediately. Yes, some things do happen overnight. But when they don't, don't let go of the good fight. Don't walk away pouting. Do what you need to do to keep going, to fight another day. That's how a child of God walks on this earth. That's how Jesus walked. Draw your strength from Him. He fought. The Greatest Man to ever walk the land had giants and battles to overcome. You're no different. Your giant may be your mouth or attitude. It may be your spending habits or pride. Whatever it is, you've got to overcome it to get to the other side. And just like God spent years preparing Jesus for the cross, He's preparing you right now for the other side. The plan for your life requires preparation. You can't just hop into it if you want to maintain it. You're asking God for much, so much is required of you. You're going to be stripped of these old ways and habits before God takes you into your promise land. But you will get there. It's yours. Nobody is taking it away. Desire what God has put in your heart. Desire what He's called you to do. Then, wait patiently for Him to bring it to pass - in His way and His timing.

**Truth Verses: James 3:14 – 16, 1 Thessalonians 5:17,
Luke 11:9 – 10, Luke 12:48, Psalm 27:14**

Beautiful Truth

Day 67

How can someone save you when they can't even save themselves? Today, quit expecting people to do what only the Lord can do. You spend so much time being mad at your family and friends thinking they should've helped you more. But they have their own struggles. Their life isn't perfect. The very area you're looking for help in could be the very area of their struggle. Maybe they can't tell you about how to maintain a good relationship because they never had one. Maybe they can't tell you about saving and making money because they don't know how. Maybe they can't tell you about raising your kids because they don't think they did a good job raising their own. You honestly have no clue what they've been through. You haven't walked in their shoes. Yes, they are your loved ones. But stop looking to them for help. Seek God for your help. He is your strength and refuge. He is the only one who can pull you out of the darkness into the marvelous light. He is your deliverer. People can't deliver you no matter how much you want them to. Real freedom from your heartache and troubles comes from the Lord. Stop putting so much pressure on the ones around you. Cut them some slack. Put your trust and faith in God to bring you through the storms and seasons of life....period.

Truth Verses: Psalm 121:1, Psalm 11:1, 1 Peter 2:9, Psalm 34:6

Beautiful Truth

Day 68

And this is the day the Lord has made. Stop letting people and situations keep you from rejoicing in it. Today, you hold the power. You don't have to react to any and everything that's going on around you. You don't have to let others make you upset and frustrated, or steal your peace. It's a choice. Nobody is "making" you mad at them. Nobody is "forcing" you to stomp around with a bad attitude. That's the choice you're making. That's what you decided to do when they said what they said or treated you like they treated you. But they're going on with their day and life while you're still rehearsing what happened. Let it go. God has blessed you with one life on this earth. You only get one shot to make it count and do the best you can. Quit wasting time and energy on foolishness, reacting to drama that happens. Life is a journey with ups and downs. Some days will be hard and difficult. It's not easy. But learn how to shake the negativity off and move on. It's one thing, one situation, one happening. It's not the end of the world. It's going to be ok and you know that. Whatever has already happened with this day, accept it and keep going. Move forward, not backward. You have plenty more days to get to in this life. Remember that.

Truth Verses: Psalm 118:24, John 14:27, Proverbs 15:18, Proverbs 29:11

Beautiful Truth

Day 69

You can be so busy doing everything for everyone else that you never do anything for yourself. Today, do you. It's that's simple. You're tired and worn out because you're putting everyone else's needs before your own. Contrary to your belief, there's nothing wrong with taking some time for yourself. There's nothing wrong with unwinding and doing the things you like to do, just relaxing. Busyness is a trick and a distraction from the enemy. He uses people, the ones closest to you, to get you off focus. Yes, it's great to give to others and to be a blessing. But that's not the only thing He created you for. You were designed with a purpose in mind. And the most important thing is to get to your purpose. What does it matter that you helped all the people in the world, but you didn't fulfill the one thing God created you to do? How is that following purpose? How is that walking in His will? It's not. Get back in line with God's plans for you. How? Take the time to regroup and refocus. Take the time to relearn what God has put in your heart to do. Spend time with Him, get to know Him again and hear His voice. You're no good to God or anyone else running around like a chicken with its head cut off. Open your eyes. Start saying "no" to the things that are draining you and get the rest and rejuvenation you need.

**Truth Verses: Ephesians 5:15 – 17, Psalm 143:10,
Jeremiah 29:13 –14, James 1:22 – 24**

Beautiful Truth

Day 70

And yes, it is. It's going to work out. Whatever you're believing God for is going to work out for your good and His glory. Today, rest in that. Quit worrying yourself silly about what could or may happen. The only thing you need to think about is God's promises coming to pass. Keep your eyes set on that. Give thanksgiving and praise about that. God is going to do what He said. He's going to deliver and bring you out. Quit thinking about what people are telling you, or what you've seen or heard them endure. You're not them. Your life is not their life. No, you're not "better" than them. But your walk and path is different. It's unique and tailor-made. Learn to accept it. Accept the goodness God is bringing to your life. Yes, you will have challenges and difficulties. But that doesn't stop God from blessing you. That doesn't mean His plans are changing. They're not. Instead of letting doubt and worry creep in, thank God for His blessings in advance. Give Him the honor for changing things in your life. Why? Because it's your praise, not your panic, that keeps God's promises moving in and through your life. Remember that.

Truth Verses: 2 Peter 3:9, Psalm 71:8, Ephesians 5:20, Isaiah 48:17

Beautiful Truth

Day 71

And did you think the enemy was just going to let you get free without a fight? Did you think it was going to be that easy? Today, anything and everything worth gaining is worth fighting for. Yes, God has called you to many blessings. Yes, there are promises with your name on it. But the enemy is just not going to let you "get" to them. He's going to throw every dart and arrow he can to stop you from inheriting the promises of God. He going to put every distraction he can in your path. He's going to pull up every dead and buried thing you've overcome. He's going to tug and pull at your emotions. He going to do everything he can to keep you down, and in the same cycle and pattern you've been in. So if you want it to change and be different, you're going to have to fight. You're going to have to push through. You're going to have to stand still and keep standing. There is no giving up. There is no quick-fix. If you want to get to everything God has for you, put your gloves on and get ready for battle. Yes, the battle is the Lord's, not yours. But you at least have to show up. You at least have to be present. You can't run away. You're too close now to get timid and afraid. Get before the Lord. Get strengthened in Him. He's your helper. You've already got the victory. But you must get in the ring and throw some punches to walk in it and see it on earth.

Truth Verses: Ephesians 6:16, 1 Corinthians 9:24 – 26, Exodus 14:13, 1 Samuel 30:6

Beautiful Truth

Day 72

Today, is it worth it? Is everything you're doing to stay in someone's good graces benefitting you? Is it making you better? Is it making the relationship or friendship stronger? Or is it slowly wearing you out? The truth is God hasn't called you to be stressed in your relationships. He wants you to blessed by others and He wants you to bless them. But when you're connected to people who are no good for you and who are bringing you down, stress is what you get. Anxiety and worry is what you find. Why? Because deep in your heart you know no matter how hard you try or what you do, it will never be good enough. They've already proven that. Sure, there are "moments" of change and hope. But it doesn't last. Real growth and change is consistent. It's not just one day. It's not just when you're upset or mad at them. It's not just when they're trying to keep you on their side. Real change keeps going. And it keeps trying. Not for you, but for the person. Quit wanting someone to change when they don't even want the change themselves. Quit wanting people to change who haven't even asked God to help them change. He's the one that can transform their heart, not you. Start recognizing who people truly are. Maybe they've been hurt. Maybe they've gone through a great tragedy and have been scarred. But until they get healed and go to the Lord for help, you're going to keep seeing and getting the same behaviors you're getting. Continue to intercede and pray for them. But how long you allow their instability and dysfunction to burden your life is your choice and consequence. Remember that.

**Truth Verses: Proverbs 27:17, Romans 12:2,
1 Corinthians 6:11, James 5:16,**

Beautiful Truth

72

Day 73

You're so busy thinking about where you're going that you forget how far you've come. Today, you're making progress. So many times you beat up on yourself thinking about what you haven't done and where you haven't made it to yet in life. But look at what you have accomplished. Look at how you're able to handle certain things better now. Look at how the people and situations that used to get under your skin no longer do. Look at what you've overcome and how you've overcome it. God has delivered and set you free. The devil can't throw those same fiery arrows at you anymore. You've changed. Yes, it's been challenging. But you made it through. You're not standing in the same place you were years ago. Be proud and celebrate that. Slow progress doesn't mean no progress. But that's what the world wants you to think. That's what people try to tell you. Yet God looks at every step you take, even small ones. And He counts it all joy. He counts it all miraculous. He is proud of every move forward you make. You should be too. There's no reason to hold your head in shame, feeling like you're not going anywhere. You are going somewhere. You're on your way to a better future, to exactly where God intends and needs you to be. Remember that.

Truth Verses: Psalm 66:9, Psalm 41:11, James 1:2, Zephaniah 3:17

Beautiful Truth

Day 74

And you keep talking about what you believe and what you've been praying for, but is it the truth? Is that really what you believe in your heart? Your actions speak louder than words. Today, put God to the test. Try Him out and see if He would not open the windows of heavens for you. Test everything you've been praying and asking for. Test everything you've been believing and standing in faith over. If God is as mighty as you profess every day, He'll work it out and resolve the matter. It'll work out in your favor. Quit letting doubt and unbelief creep into your head. That's what's causing your actions not to line up with your prayers. That's what's causing you to walk in fear instead of faith. God didn't bring you this far to just drop you off and leave you. He has a plan and a purpose. Just because you can't see or understand it right now doesn't mean it's not working. And just because you can't see or control it doesn't mean you take matters into your own hands. It doesn't mean you begin doing things yourself out of fear while calling them acts of faith. A true act of faith is resting in the finished works of Jesus. Everything you're believing and praying for is already done. It is finished. Act like it. How? Thank God for it. Instead of trying to piece things together in your own mind and make them work, thank God for making them work. Thank God that it's in His precious, capable hands. Thank God for doing what you can't do on your own. Yes, you have the power and authority in you. But only God can do what you can't.

Truth Verses: Malachi 3:10, John 11:40, 2 Corinthians 4:18

Beautiful Truth

Day 75

And if you didn't have it so bad back then you wouldn't know what it's like to have it so good now. Today, appreciate the mess God brought you out of. Quit complaining about it. Quit saying how awful and how terrible it was. Yes, it was miserable. Sure, it nearly destroyed you. But what did you learn from it? Some people go through life and never learn anything. Why? Because they haven't experienced the ups and downs of life. So when a bad situation approaches them, they can't discern that it isn't good for them. When a relationship or someone comes their way that isn't beneficial, they can't see the downfall of it. They don't have wisdom in that area because they haven't experienced it. But you do. Be thankful about that. That means you don't have to spend the rest of your life going around the same mountain. That means you know the voice of the Lord and know what to do when. You won't harden your heart. You won't hurry along to the first thing that looks good. You've learned to wait on the Lord. You've learned to press through. You've learned about yourself and what you're weak to. Be ok with that. Stop feeling bad about the challenges you've had in life. Have they stopped your progress? No. You've been able to keep going and get to the other side. That's maturity and growth. That's wisdom. See it as such.

Truth Verses: Leviticus 26:13, Proverbs 3:13 – 15, Psalm 95:8, Luke 2:40

Beautiful Truth

Day 76

Honestly, nobody can tell you what you need to do in every situation. Sometimes, you will just have to figure it out on your own. Today, you're wise and smart enough to know what the answer is to this problem. Quit doubting yourself. The Holy Spirit is in you. Christ is in you. You have His leading, guiding and voice down on the inside of you. You know when He's leading you to something. Sure, this situation is something you haven't been challenged with or up against before. Sure, you're afraid. But much is given, much is required. God isn't looking to bless your stagnancy. He isn't looking to bless the same thing you've been doing that hasn't been working. He's looking to bless what you're willing to step out and trust Him on. In this situation, no matter what you decide to do, it will require your faith and reliance on God. It doesn't require what others know and believe, but what you believe yourself. It requires what you know and believe about your Heavenly Father. Get confident in knowing His character. Get confident in knowing how He leads and guides you. God isn't going to lead you astray on this decision. You're going to know exactly what to do when. And if you don't, keep waiting on Him until you do know what to do. You don't need the advice of others. You need to know what to do for yourself by the grace of God. Remember that.

Truth Verses: John 14:26, John 15:3 – 4, Proverbs 3:6 – 7, Isaiah 30:21

Beautiful Truth

Day 77

And maybe God allowed you to go through it so you could help someone else. It's not always about you. Today, your greatest pain could be the greatest blessing to someone else. The thing that took so much out of you and nearly destroyed you could be the very thing that will save someone else's life. Don't discredit that. Don't take for granted the dark days you've had, the peaks and valleys you've been through. It wasn't in vain. Yes, it was the greatest challenge of your life. It was difficult. But you made it through for a reason. You lived to tell and share it. Your test is now your testimony. What the enemy intended for bad, God used for good. He used it to bless you and someone else in the long run. It may not feel like a blessing. But the truth is it shaped and molded you. As hard as it was, it helped you become the strong person you are. Don't knock that. Instead of being angry about it, find the peace of God in it. Yes, it's hard to do. But there's light in that dark tunnel. There's shimmer in that gloom. Find it. Then, ask God to help you use it for His good and glory.

Truth Verses: Isaiah 61:1 – 3, Psalm 23:4, Isaiah 42:16, Genesis 50:20

Beautiful Truth

Day 78

Who cares what "they" have to say? What does God say? Today, remember who you are serving. God didn't put you in this world to seek the approval of people. Everything you do is unto the Lord. Every word you speak and move you make is in service to Him. Quit worrying about who is or isn't going to understand the things He's called you to. The truth is everybody around you will not understand your plight. Nor will they support it. They will not understand your journey or even like it. Some people will only be there to stop you from moving forward. They want to hold you back. They want you to be in the same situation they're in. It's a trick of the enemy. There will always be someone who will try to tear you down and make you feel bad about yourself or what you're doing. But if God has called you to it, nobody else has a say in it...period. Stop letting these people speak into your life and destroy your progress. Stop giving them your ear and your time. Is what they are saying valuable? Does it sound like the voice of God? Is it something He would say or tell you to do? No. Then, don't feed on their words. Feed on God's word. Meditate on His promises. Get those in your heart and spirit. Get the trash out of your life. Disconnect from people who are filling your head with the wrong things. They're bringing no value to your life or spirit. You know it and God knows it. And it's time for you to do something about it.

Truth Verses: Colossians 3:17, Colossians 3:23, 1 Corinthians 2:14, Philippians 4:8

Beautiful Truth

Day 79

You can't get to God's goodness by holding on to what's familiar. It doesn't work like that. Today, God operates in faith, in those things you hope for but can't yet see. He operates in you stepping out and trusting Him enough to go forward. Nothing you desire in this life will come without faith. For without faith, it is impossible to please God. With every blessing God gives you, your faith will be tested on it before you receive it. He will not allow you to hold on to what's comfortable and convenient while you simultaneously reach and grab for the things that are ahead. How is that faith? How is it true belief if you can hold tight to what you have while obtaining what you don't have? It's not. Real faith is letting go. It's trusting that if you let go, when you let go, God's got you. It's knowing that He's not going to let anything happen to you. He will intentionally work the situation out for your good and His glory, even if it doesn't turn out like you expected. So stop being afraid of what you're losing. Have a vision for what you're gaining. Is the situation you're in so wonderful and great that you can't risk letting it go? Are you growing that much in it? If you're not growing in the things of God, why are staying in this dead-end situation? It's called being stagnant. Learn how to walk fully in the things of God. Put yourself out there. Get out of the boat and walk on water. Walk to Jesus in this situation. You won't fall. Keep your eyes on your Savior and trust in Him. Do what you have to do and take the risk today. Step out on faith.

Truth Verses: Hebrews 11:1, Hebrews 11:6, Psalm 121:3, Matthew 14:29

Beautiful Truth

Day 80

You can't make anyone "get it." God will help them see what they need to see or they won't see it at all. Today, it's not your job to bring people to their "other side," to their land of milk and honey. Yes, your heart is in the right place and you want people to be and do better. But the revelation God has given you about life, His promises, and how to obtain them won't always make sense to other people. Is He revealing the same thing to you that He is to them? Maybe. But that doesn't mean they're always listening. And neither do you listen always. But when you're obedient to God, you can't be held back in your walk and progress because the people you love aren't following God's plans and ways. It doesn't mean you're better than them. It just means you're choosing to listen to the Word of the Lord so your outcome in life will be different. It means you may have to leave the ones you love behind or change how you interact with them to pursue and obtain the promises of God. Quit feeling bad about it. You're not their keeper, God is. You're an intercessor on their behalf. You can go to God in prayer for them. You can stand in faith with them. But out here in this world, they must put their own actions forth. They must put their own foot forward for their life. It's not on you. Remember that.

Truth Verses: Deuteronomy 32:39, Isaiah 42:20,
Matthew 7:24 – 25, 1 Timothy 2:1

Beautiful Truth

Day 81

The truth is you don't want to go through anything difficult or hard in this life. You expect to go through life easy and without pain just because you serve God. But God hasn't promised you "easy" because you serve Him. He's promised you that through Him you can overcome and get through all things. Today, you can and will get through this. Believe that. Every challenge or battle you've been up against you've won. And it wasn't because of your doing. It was because of the Lord's. It was because He was on your side. It was because He gave you the strength. It was because He pushed you when you wanted to give up. Not by your might or power, but by His spirit. And it's going to be the same way now. How you get through this difficulty and uncertainty is not by running away or avoiding it. You face it head on, but with God. The enemy wants you to run scared. He wants you to think "you" have to fix it. But you don't. You can't. You're facing it with God. You're not alone. You face everything in this life with Him. He has your back. So no matter what comes up today, tomorrow or whenever, you're able to withstand it. You'll cross every bridge when you get to it, and God will be right there with you. Remember that.

**Truth Verses: Philippians 4:13, Zechariah 4:6,
Hebrews 13:6, Deuteronomy 31:8**

Beautiful Truth

Day 82

And you could have a beautiful life too. But you're so focused on what you didn't get in the past that you can't see the beauty of your future. Today, look forward, not backward. Contrary to your belief and feelings, you didn't miss out on anything. You didn't get the short end of the stick. What you got was what you were supposed to get. Sure, it may have hurt you. But you came out on top. How? You're still here. You're still standing. What was supposed to take you out didn't. What was supposed to kill you, couldn't. What was supposed to tear you apart and destroy you, didn't touch you. That's a victory, child of God. That's winning. Too many times you look back on your life and see the things you didn't get or the people who didn't stay with you as a loss. But it's not a loss. It's a gain. Whoever and whatever walked out of your life by choice was God's blessing to you. It was not a burden or punishment. It was God shining down on you. He's been dedicated to you all your life. He will never leave you for any reason or circumstance. That's how much He loves and adores you. If someone can't show that same type of commitment to you, they're not of God. They're not loving you like Christ loves you. And you don't need that type of instability. You deserve better than that. Quit looking back. This is a new day. And if you're still living and breathing, God has greater and better in store for you. Fight for your bright future today. Fight for what's next. Fight for the life Christ died for you to have.

Truth Verses: Psalm 126:5, Ephesians 5:1 – 2, Isaiah 42:9, John 10:10

Beautiful Truth

Day 83

And "what if, what if, what if?" What if all your "what ifs" are completely wrong? Today, quit telling God what you think. Haven't you figured out by now that as much as you tell God what you think, He's going to do what's best for you anyway? God doesn't mind your opinions. He wants to give you the desires of your heart. But He also knows your desires could be wrong. He knows what you want may not always be what's good for you. Why? Because you only see what you want at this very moment. You only look at your experiences and what you've been through. You only see the bad and that you want to get out of your situation. But God doesn't always deliver you in the way you want or in the time you want. He sees your end from the beginning and He delivers you according to what's best for you. Quit being so shut down and closed off. The enemy has hardened your heart. He's made you believe everything you encounter from now on will be as bad as it was before. But it won't. Let God show you different. He makes all things new. He's able to give you a new heart and spirit. He's able to take the bad and turn it into good. Don't limit God today. Believe Him enough to do the impossible. Trust that what He's telling you to do is best and be open to His spirit.

**Truth Verses: Isaiah 46:10, Revelation 21:5,
Ezekiel 36:26, Matthew 19:26**

Beautiful Truth

Day 84

You're not in competition with anyone. What God is doing in someone else's life has absolutely nothing to do with you. Today, stay focused on your own life. God has a plan and purpose for you. And whatever you're doing that's not on His plan is a distraction. Getting involved in other people's business is a distraction. Worrying about what they're doing and why is a distraction. Trying to figure out why they're getting blessed in a certain area and you're not is a distraction. That's not what God has called you to. You were not made to compare yourself to others. You were made to be you. You're not supposed to be in competition with anyone. This is why you're frustrated and discouraged, upset about your own life and what's in it. You don't see the gifts and talents God has given you. You only see what He's given to someone else. Stop it. We all are blessed with gifts. But just because it's not what someone else has doesn't mean you're inadequate. It doesn't mean you're in lack. You're just as great as the next man. You have just as much to offer. Quit looking down on yourself, thinking what you have isn't good enough. You've been blessed with much. And contrary to your belief, it is good enough. It's exactly what you need.

Truth Verses: Jeremiah 29:11, 1 Corinthians 12:4 – 6, Ephesians 1:3

Beautiful Truth

Day 85

You can't keep using guilt to make people stay and be connected to you. Either they will love you for who you are or they won't love you at all. Today, you are more than enough. You don't have to manipulate somebody into staying with you. You don't have to trick or deceive them into being in your life. You are fearfully and wonderfully created by God. You're a precious jewel, a diamond in the rough. Just because somebody doesn't realize that doesn't mean you need to devalue yourself. You don't lessen who you are and what you bring to the table because someone can't see the rare treasure they have in their possession. You don't need to grovel, beg or be less than who God created you to be to stay in their good graces or to have a relationship. There are millions of people in this world. Do you think God put you here on this earth and wouldn't supply you with the relationships and friendships you need? Do you think He placed you in your town, job, community and church, but there's nobody there to embrace, love and care for you? The devil is a liar. Quit believing his words. God loves you more than anything in this world. And He loves you just as you are. Find people like that to be in your corner. Share your world and time with people that love and treat you like Christ does. It's not just a fantasy or a dream. There are good people out here who will treat you like you need. And you don't have to manipulate, change or chase behind them to make it happen. They will truly value and appreciate the type of person you are. Allow God to lead you to them.

Truth Verses: Ephesians 5:29, Ephesians 2:10, Galatians 1:10

Beautiful Truth

Day 86

And it's not for you to worry about. If you could truly do something about it, you would. But you can't. This situation is on God, not you. Today, take a deep breath. This is not your battle or problem to solve. You've gotten yourself stressed out over something you have no control over. Did you get yourself into this? Did you bring this situation into your life? No. If you had nothing to do with the creation of it, then you have nothing to do with the resolve. Just like a product that breaks down, only the manufacturer can fix it. Only someone specially trained in that area can make it work and make it brand new. As smart as you "think" you are, you're not skilled in this area. This isn't your field. You're not cut out for the work that has to be done here. Let God handle it. He is your Manufacturer. He's your fixer. You can't figure this thing out on your own. Trust in the Lord. That's the answer to this problem. Instead of trying to figure out the next step or the right thing to do, open your mouth and tell the Lord "help". Tell Him you need His help to turn the situation over to Him. Tell Him you need His guidance. Tell Him to help you stop worrying. Worrying is the most powerless thing you can do. But when you call on the name of Jesus and seek His face, your power shows up. That's when you see the hand of the Lord working.

Truth Verses: Matthew 6:28, Matthew 6:34, Isaiah 54:10, Psalm 25:4

Beautiful Truth

Day 87

"New" and "different" doesn't always mean bad. It's just that you're not used to it. Today, there's nothing wrong with the new thing God is doing in your life. You didn't make a mistake or the wrong decision. You haven't gotten off the path. It's just new. That's all. And with every new blessing, there are new challenges. Your problem is you're so used to the old way of doing things, even though it was broken and dysfunctional, you can't see how this newness is going to be any better. You're so stuck in the familiar that you're making a mountain out of a molehill. Stop it. This blessing is what you prayed and asked God for. And now that it's here, you're stressing about it? Don't make the situation more than what it is. Handle it. You're more than a conqueror in Christ. Just because it's what you wanted doesn't mean it's coming on a silver platter. It doesn't mean it's going to be easy. God never promised you that. But He did allow this opportunity into your life because He knows you're equipped and ready. He knows you can do this. He's with you. Trust that. As long as God's with you, you'll be successful. As long as He's with you, you'll get the answers and direction you need. You won't have to do everything on your own or in your own strength. You'll have the help and strength you need in this new world and environment you've entered. Remember that.

Truth Verses: Matthew 9:17, Ephesians 3:16, Isaiah 41:13

Beautiful Truth

Day 88

Some things you're going to have to let go of. Everything that's good to you isn't good for you. Today, what is the priority? What are you really supposed to be doing? The biggest trick of the enemy is distraction. If he can keep you from doing what you're called to do, he will. If he can keep you distracted with activities, people, and things, he will. If he can keep you in guilt, always feeling bad about who you can't help and what you don't have time for, he will. He'll make you feel obligated to people and things God never called you to be tied to. It's a trick. He wants you off your game. He wants you so far off what God has for you that you never get it back. That's his plan for your life - to slowly, but surely destroy you. Beat him at his own game. How? Ask God for guidance. You have not, because you ask not. You don't know how your steps need to be ordered because you don't ask for it. You don't know what should or shouldn't be on your plate because you aren't seeking it. The answer isn't just going to come to you. God isn't going to just drop it down from the sky. You must seek and desire the will of God for your life. You must seek and desire to be in line with His priorities. God isn't going to force His ways on you. Start seeking them out. Ask God to help you prioritize your days. Ask Him what things are most important. Ask Him who and what to make time for. Then, you'll know what's valuable and what's not.

Truth Verses: 2 Corinthians 2:11, Jeremiah 29:13, 1 John 5:14

Beautiful Truth

Day 89

And if you can't clearly hear from God, you have no direction. You can't just jump out there and "see how it goes." Today, wait patiently on the Lord. Yes, you want to move on to the next step. Sure, this "feels" right for you. But is it? Is this truly the best thing for you to do? If you can't answer that question with confidence, you can't move. You can't launch out into the deep. You can't say "this is the way." Yes, God wants you to step out in faith, walk in new ways, and try things you haven't before. But God guides you in peace. You may feel nervous and anxious about doing something new. But that's your emotions and nerves. They have nothing to do with a lack of peace. A real lack of peace doesn't go away. After your nerves calm down, it's still there. It doesn't leave because it's an indicator of what God doesn't want you to do. Pay attention to that. Stop ignoring it. That's His Holy Spirit guiding you. You can do a lot of things in this world. You can take a lot of risks and walk into a lot of new adventures. But if God isn't in them, they won't work out well. Why? Because His favor and grace won't be there. Stop trying to push through this unsettling vibe you keep getting. Instead, trust in it. Trust that God is in you and you're in Him. That through the lack of peace you're feeling, He's speaking to you. Listen closely. That'll be enough to give you all the guidance you need.

Truth Verses: Isaiah 28:23, 1 Corinthians 14:33, John 14:20

Beautiful Truth

Day 90

⌒~⌒

And no, you don't know. You don't how the situation will turn out until you walk through it. Today, it's a process. Quit shutting down the possibility before it even rises. Too many times God is looking to bless you with the very thing you're asking for, but you shut it down with your fear. You stop the miracle before it starts with your doubt. The truth is you don't know half of what you think you know. Just because you've been through a lot doesn't mean you've been through everything. You haven't seen it all. Yes, you have wisdom and have gained knowledge. But that doesn't mean you have insight on every particular matter. Only God does. Only He is the first and last in every situation. Stop being so closed minded. You talk a good game and quote that God can do anything. Well, believe Him to do this. Believe Him to handle this situation for you. Believe Him to take care of you and show you kindness. Just because things look "gloom and doom" doesn't mean they truly are. You have the power and authority to change anything you see that's not lining up with God's word and goodness for you. Instead of living with it, speak to it. Open your mouth and tell fear where to go. Tell doubt it has no place in your life. Tell worry you're trusting God. That's how you walk in the opportunities of a lifetime. That's how you go from thinking you know it all to walking full of faith, completely trusting God. You stop the pride, unbelief and distrust from getting into your ear.

Truth Verses: Psalm 115:11, Isaiah 48:3, Isaiah 41:4, Mark 11:23

Beautiful Truth

Day 91

Just because it happened to someone else doesn't mean it'll happen to you. Today, stop being so fearful. Stop being so afraid to live your life because you think it'll turn out like somebody else's. Is your name their name? Are you walking in their shoes, living in their body, living out their life? No. Then, why are you comparing yourself to them? Why are you looking at what they're doing and assuming it will be the same for you? It won't. You're different. God created you in His image from your mother's womb with a specific destiny in mind. He didn't bring you into this world attached to anyone else. Because of that, whether bad or good, what has happened to someone else has nothing to do with you. It can't change the plan God has for your life. Your plan has already been created. It's set in stone. Nothing anyone tries to do can change that. God isn't in Heaven changing what He's planned for you because someone else couldn't handle the blessings He gave them. God's blessings are individual, not universal. Yes, He is no respecter of persons. Sure, the blessings He provides to one person He can provide to another. But what each person chooses to do with that blessing is their individual choice and decision. God is not regulating your decisions. Nor is He forcing you to do anything. You have free will. God has put before you blessings and curses, life and death. He says choose. He says to make a decision. Start seeing your life like this. Your decisions don't belong to anyone else but you. Yes, people are impacted by what you do. But the power to make a choice is yours and yours only. And so is the consequence.

**Truth Verses: Psalm 112:7, Psalm 139:13,
Romans 2:11, Deuteronomy 30:19**

Beautiful Truth

Day 92

No matter how hard you try, there are some things you're just weak to. And God understands that. But just because you're weak to a thing doesn't mean you let it rule your life. Whether it's a thing or a person, you don't roll over and accept it when you know it's no good for you. Today, keep fighting. Sure, you're tired of battling this thing. Yes, you're worn out from wrestling and trying to overcome it. But you're exhausted because you've been fighting this battle in the wrong way. You've been trying to stand strong against temptations in your own strength. You've been telling yourself every day you're over it and that because you're not around it anymore, you've won the battle. But if the devil can still tempt you with it, you haven't won anything. He can't tempt you with what you're truly over. The truth is this person or situation still has a hold on you. Just because you've walked away doesn't mean it's destroyed. So how do you destroy it? Give it over to God completely. How? Admit you're weak to it. Admit you still desire it. Be honest. Quit hiding from it. The devil can't hold darkness over you when you expose it to the light. This issue is your weakness, your Achilles Heel. But God is your strength. In your weakness, He gives you the grace to be strong when you rely on Him. In your weakness, He keeps you uplifted when you remain close to Him. And that's the key to your breakthrough - staying connected to God at all times. Your real deliverance has nothing to do with you and how tough you think you are. It's in you seeing how weak you truly are, but looking to God to carry you. It's called being humble unto the Lord.

**Truth Verses: Hebrews 2:18, Matthew 26:41,
Hebrews 4:15 – 16, James 4:7**

Beautiful Truth

Day 93

All of Him, none of you. Today, die to yourself. When you accepted Christ and chose Jesus as Lord over your life, you let go of you. You walked away from what you wanted, how and when. It was no longer about you. Now, everything you do and everything you are is for God. Every word you speak and step you take is about glorifying His name and being in His presence. Sure, God cares about your concerns and desires. But He wants your desires to be His desires. He wants your wants to be His wants. That's what dying to yourself is. It's you sacrificing what you want for Him. It's you purposely and consciously saying "Lord, Your will be done," each day of your life. Yes, it sounds good, but are you willing to do it? Are you truly willing to kill your passions and desires to let God rule and reign in your life? Do you truly want Him to be Lord over your life, circumstances and all that you are? If you don't mean it, don't commit to it. Don't speak it just because it sounds good. God isn't about hearing a bunch of empty promises. He desires all of you, including your words and actions, to be submitted to Him. Quit talking about it and start being about it. Put some action behind what you're quoting and living for. If you've truly chosen to live for Christ, let Him lead and guide you in all areas of your life, including your speech, relationships and the places you go.

Truth Verses: Galatians 2:20, Luke 9:23 – 24, Romans 6:11

Beautiful Truth

Day 94

Sometimes God will allow the test and trial just to see how you will handle it. Why? Because if you can't handle the small and minor disturbances that come your way and give them over to God, how will you turn to Him when the large, pressing disasters come into your life? You won't. Today, it's all about how you handle it. God isn't looking for a perfect person. He isn't looking for the person who behaves and handles everything right, without getting frustrated or angry. He knows certain things will get under your skin. He knows certain people and situations will cause you to falter or get out of character. But just because He understands it doesn't mean He wants you to keep doing it. It doesn't mean that's His best for you. What God wants for you is to rely on Him at all times in all circumstances. That's how you navigate through this life. That's how you bypass the tests and storms. That's how you overcome and win. It's not by your perfect behavior. Yes, God wants you to walk in the spirit and display His Godly nature. But He knows you sin and fall short. Because of that, His expectation of you isn't perfectionism. It's to remain close to Him. It's your dependence on Him that keeps you from falling and going off the deep end. You alone are too fragile to handle these challenges in life. But through God's presence and protection, through His wisdom, help and Holy Spirit – you can handle all things that come your way. That's how you gain true peace and ease in your life.

**Truth Verses: Isaiah 26:4, Romans 3:23, John 15:4 – 5,
Philippians 4:13**

Beautiful Truth

Day 95

At the end of the day, you must do what's best for you. You can't be concerned with what people are saying or how they perceive you. Today, this is your life. Live it. Quit being so paranoid and focused on what someone will say about what you're choosing to do. Are you following God? Do you believe this is the path He's chosen for you? Then, that settles it. There are no "if, ands, or buts." There is no second-guessing or letting others chime in. God has spoken. He is the ruler of your life. He is the manager of your days. Sure, people can have an opinion. God will even use them to speak to you. But their word isn't what you base your life and decisions on. Their word isn't final. God's is. Know the voice of the Lord and follow it. Take heed. Seek and listen to it. God's words don't have to make sense to your family and friends. They don't even have to make sense to you. But let the peace of God rule and reign in your heart and mind – not what everyone else is telling you to do. Seek His will and direction for your life. If that's what you have, that's all you need. The rest is nothing more than a distraction. Remember that.

Truth Verses: Deuteronomy 10:12 – 13, John 10:27, Colossians 3:15

Beautiful Truth

Day 96

And it's nothing that can't be fixed. Today, there is a solution. As hard as it is, stop panicking. God isn't going to leave you stuck. He's not going to leave you down and out. He loves you. Just because trouble has come doesn't mean God isn't on the scene. He already has the answer to your problem. And you will see it. When? When you need to. Right now, quit focusing on that. This is what makes you worried and stressed. The time and the day of deliverance shouldn't be your focus. Focus on the promise. That's what provides peace in the storm. That's what provides joy in the chaos. What is the promise? That God won't leave you in this. He won't leave you like this. He will provide a way out, the best solution possible. Stop looking to and holding on to the "how" and "when." Stop holding on to how you think it should go and what you want to happen. It's not about you. When you choose to cast your care to God, you give up your wants. You trust that He's heard your prayers and He will give you the desires of your heart – more than you could've ever wanted, needed or asked for. Learn how to live your life like this. Stop stressing yourself out. God's got it under control. Go ahead with your day and rest assured of that.

Truth Verses: Genesis 28:15, Psalm 138:3, Isaiah 55:11, Psalm 37:4

Beautiful Truth

Day 97

And it won't always be like this. Today, this season won't last always. This is not your entire life. This is not "it." God has more in store for you. He has something better. It's on the other side of this mountain, the one you keep going around. Sure, it may not feel like it. Yes, it's been a long time coming. But God is a god of the "and suddenly". In one moment, He can turn your darkness to light. In one second, your miracle can come into being. Quit thinking right now is all there is. That's what the enemy wants you to think. That's what he wants you to believe. Why? Because if you don't believe for change, it won't happen. It'll never come. Change happens when you have the faith for it. Your situation turns around when you believe it will. Start believing for it. Your life is not always going to be this hard or difficult. Jesus didn't come for that. Yes, you have challenging circumstances to face. But your life isn't supposed to be an uphill battle all the time. Difficulty and trouble shouldn't plague you constantly. The devil is a liar. You have the victory. Christ has already won so that you may have life and have it in abundance. That's your aim and goal. Don't look at where you are now. Walk with and trust God enough to get to your blessed future.

Truth Verses: Isaiah 42:16, Hebrews 11:1, Numbers 13:27 – 30

Day 98

Somebody will always have something to say about you. They'll love you one minute and hate you the next. It happens. But what you must do is get up each day and be confident in who you are and in who God called you to be. Every day you rise, you must know you are doing the best you can and are being the best you can be. Today, quit letting people's thoughts about you rock your world. Stop letting their words shape and define you. The enemy knows how to get to you. He knows who to use and how. He knows the very thing to make someone say or do to make you feel rejected. He knows how to make you feel like you're not good enough, smart enough, good looking enough, or qualified enough. But the devil is a liar. God is your judge, not the enemy or man. God's the one who created you for His purpose. He's the one that formed you in your mother's womb. He's the one that has stood by you. And if He's not displeased with you, why are you listening to other people who don't even really know you? Why are you letting what your family, friends and even strangers say, upset you? Why are you giving them that much weight and attention in your life? Stop it. Learn how not to react to it. Learn how to sense through the Holy Spirit what is unwise or negative talk coming out of people's mouth. Flee from it. Yes, words are hurtful and make you feel bad about yourself. But aren't you tired of letting people control you, allowing them to make you feel up one moment and down the next? Remain steadfast in feeling good about yourself. You're a child of God, fearfully and wonderfully made, exceptional on the inside and out. Stop doubting yourself. Everyone will not be your cheerleader. But for every person that has something negative to say and that is not in your corner, God will bring and have that many more who are in your corner. Remember that.

Truth Verses: Psalm 146:3, Ephesians 2:10, Psalm 8:4 – 5, Proverbs 15:14

Beautiful Truth

Day 99

You're not responsible for other people. Yes, you can help them. But it's not your job to lift the weight off their back. How can you lift theirs when you can't even lift your own? Today, quit putting extra pressure on yourself. People will wear you out with their worries and troubles. They'll drive you crazy with their issues and problems. Sure, you're supposed to be there and help others. But it shouldn't get in the way of your own affairs. It shouldn't keep you from being focused on your own family, job, house, or other priorities. Contrary to your belief, you're not called to be people's savior. God is. Point them in the direction of the Lord. That's the advice you need to give them. That's the support you need to provide. God is their answer, not you. He is their refuge and peace, not you. You can't solve their issues. And listening to them repeatedly is draining and stressing you. It's making you resentful and angry. And God doesn't need you resenting others. He needs you to be helpful. But you can't be helpful when you don't know how to draw a line in the sand. Set better boundaries with others. If helping them is draining and distracting you, it's taking away from your life. It's not adding to it. Get your priorities back in order. You don't need anyone or anything pulling from you. You need to be focused and alert on what God has for you. It's not selfish. It's just where your attention needs to be right now.

Truth Verses: Exodus 18:14 – 20, Psalm 50:6,
2 Thessalonians 3:11 – 12 (NLT)

Beautiful Truth

Day 100

If God led you to it, He's going to get you through it. Today, God didn't place you where you are to leave you. Remember that. Too many times you panic when things don't line up the way you planned. But what you must remember is that if God has given you the grace for the situation and has ordained for you to be where you are, He's got you. He's not going to leave you in lack. That's the enemy filling your head with doubt and fear. That's you looking at what has happened to someone else. Regardless of what happened to another person, you're not them. God is protecting and keeping you. He's not going to supply you with His blessing, but not give you the provision to sustain it. Nor is He going to take it away. He trusts you with His blessings and gifts. Sure, you're not perfect. But your behavior and mistakes have nothing to do with God's faithfulness. He's faithful regardless of your actions or the circumstance. Quit worrying. God promised in His word that He would supply all your needs according to His riches and glory. Stand on that promise. Walk in it. Stop allowing your mind to run rampant with these anxious thoughts. God is for you, with you and He loves you. Challenges may come, but whatever it is, whenever it comes, it's not going to prosper against you. God will make sure you're taken care of.

Truth Verses: Psalm 17:5, Philippians 4:19, Isaiah 54:17

Beautiful Truth

Day 101

Just because it's what you want to do doesn't mean it's what you're called to do. Today, are you really supposed to be doing what you're doing? Is this relationship, job, career, or venture what God has truly called you to? If so, why are you so stressed out? Why are you ready to give up and throw in the towel? The true promises of God stretch you, not stress you. They don't have you losing sleep and peace. They don't have you up and down, happy one minute, sad the next. They don't have you getting out of line and out of character. The things God has called you to grow you. They develop and shape you. They make you stronger, never weaker. Yes, the promises of God are hard and challenging. But you can still have peace and joy in the midst of them. Why? Because you're confident in what the Lord told you. Start examining your life this way. Is what you're putting all your might and strength into helping or hurting you? Did God honestly tell you to pursue it or did you just do what you wanted? There's a difference. God's callings are sweat less victories. They are victories through grace and favor, triumphs without stress and resentment. Why? Because there is a knowing deep, down inside that this is God's will and plan for you. That's what keeps you grounded and at ease. That's what provides the grace you need to keep going. Remember that.

Truth Verses: 2 Peter 1:10, Proverbs 16:9, Philippians 1:6

Beautiful Truth

Day 102

And God's plans for your life will come to pass. You can go kicking and screaming, or you can be obedient and submit. Today, which will it be? The truth is you have no real control over your life. You can't control what happens, how or when. No matter how much you think you're ruling your life, you're not. God can interrupt your plans at any time. He can change the course and path whenever He likes. But because He loves you, He gives you free will. You have a choice. But that doesn't mean you're the master of your fate. That doesn't mean you're running the show or are in charge of it all. God's in charge. He's the master. He's the ruler and king of your castle. And when you agreed to let Him lead your life, you gave up your rights, plans, and ways. Your only plan now is to submit. Learn how to do just that. God isn't trying to hurt you or make you suffer. He sees the things you can't see. He sees what's best and right for you. Open your eyes to it. Not to the situation, but to God. You don't need to understand everything that's going on. God is your eyes and ears. He's leading and guiding you. He has your back. Instead of putting up resistance towards His plan, trust it. God knows what He's doing. He's been good to you. If He kept you before, He'll do it again. You just have to surrender all. Are you ready?

Truth Verses: Proverbs 14:12, James 4:10, Matthew 16:24, Revelation 11:17, Hebrews 13:8

Beautiful Truth

Day 103

You win some. You lose some. But at least you put yourself out there. At least you took the chance. Today, the only failure in this life is never trying at all. It's allowing the enemy to get so far into your head that you become too fearful and afraid to even attempt the things God has placed in your heart. The truth is everything God puts in your heart will cause fear and panic. Why? Because it's too big for you to carry alone. That's how you know it's from God. If you could do it in your own strength and might, what would you need God for? Why would you need prayer or faith? You wouldn't. On your own, you can't see how things will shape out or come to pass. You can't fathom why God would use you. But it's not about your understanding. It's about your obedience. Just follow. That's all God is asking you to do. And if following causes you to lose sometimes, it's ok. It doesn't mean your life or story is over. It's not. Learn how to keep going. God is never upset that things didn't go as you planned. You stepped out, didn't you? That alone shows Him where your trust is. That alone shows Him where your faith is. Stop allowing these setbacks to define you, or to make you think differently about yourself and God. You're His child. You're blessed and highly favored regardless. No setback or obstacle is changing that.

Truth Verses: Zechariah 4:6, Haggi 2:4, Proverbs 3:5, Numbers 23:19

Beautiful Truth

Day 104

And the Holy Spirit is here to guide and help you answer the questions you can't answer. Today, are you using Him? Too many times you claim "I don't know what to do," but you haven't asked the Holy Spirit, your helper, to assist you. You're asking family and friends. You're listening to what's on TV. You're turning to social media. You're searching the Internet, but you're not asking the One who truly knows. The truth is nobody knows you or your situation like Jesus. Nobody knows what you need or what's coming down the road, but God. Quit going to other people or just sitting there feeling confused. God is not a God of confusion, but of peace. You don't have to be confused. You're choosing to. God has the answer about everything in your life. And the Holy Spirit will guide you to it, but you must seek Him out. You have to be humble enough to ask. You have to be wise enough to know you need help. God gives grace to the humble, which means He provides His help to those who say "Lord, I don't know what I'm doing. I don't know which way to go, but I know You do." That's when God comes to the rescue, not when you sit there, debating things back and forth in your head. It's not when you go to everyone else or try to keep your feelings to yourself. God can't do anything with that. But when you open up to Him, when you start asking the Holy Spirit about everything in your life, He can move mountains. Speak to Him today like you would anyone else. From purchasing a car to who to marry, the Holy Spirit wants to be a part of it all. Jesus died to save you. He sent the Holy Spirit to help you. Use Him today.

Truth Verses: 1 Corinthians 14:33, Proverbs 3:34, John 16:7, John 14:26

Beautiful Truth

Day 105

Perhaps the reason you feel disconnected and like you can't hear from God is because you're doing too much. Today, slow yourself down. You have time. The things God has ordained for to do aren't going anywhere. You don't have to beat some invisible clock. You don't have to rush around, trying to complete everything. Stop putting so much pressure on yourself. What are you trying to prove? Who are you trying to prove it to? You piling more on your plate isn't helping you. It isn't impressing or pleasing God. It actually displeases Him. It hurts Him. Why? Because He loves you. And He hates seeing you try to do things in your own strength. He hates watching you force or try to make things happen in your life. That's not what God intended for you. He's here to help you. He made Himself available so you could rely on Him, not on your own thoughts, ideas and plans. He's your help so you don't have to feel this struggle and strain you're feeling. Give God a chance to rule in your life. When was the last time you actually let Him lead you? When was the last time you actually gave Him your day, time and schedule? When was the last time you said "My plans don't matter. What do you want me to focus on, Lord?" This is how you begin connecting with Him and hearing from Him, seeing His presence in your life. You can't recognize what He's doing when you're too busy to pay attention. You can't sense His presence when you're focused on other things and people. Give yourself a break today. God is more important than any task you have to do. Put Him back first in your life and everything else will fall into place.

Truth Verses: Ecclesiastes 8:6, Psalm 31:3, Luke 10:42, Luke 12:31

Beautiful Truth

Day 106

~⟡

And if this is the best you can do, why are you trying to do anything else? Why are you trying to squeeze more out of yourself? Today, leave well enough alone. You're stressing yourself out to the point of no return. You're doing all these things for all these people, but you're wearing yourself out. The truth is you running around doing so much is not even to please God, but to please people. It's the people in your life you feel obligated and committed to. It's the people in your life you feel you can't let down or you need to be responsible for. But you're not responsible for them. God is. Just like God is taking care of you every day, He's taking care of them. He's giving them their daily bread. He's making a way out of no way. He's supplying their needs. Just because it's not necessarily what they want or how they think it should be doesn't mean God's not working on their behalf. Nor does it mean it's your job to come in and save the day. Let God be responsible for other people. Yes, you should help people when you can. But lending a hand shouldn't cause you to neglect the things God has assigned for you to do. Stop allowing people to distract you. Stop stretching yourself thin to make others happy. If you're not happy and full of peace while you're helping someone, how is it effective? How are you truly doing good? You're not. If your heart isn't in it, you're doing nothing more than just empty works. Learn how to set the proper boundaries so you can be a light and vessel to others, without the angst and frustration. You can honestly do no good to yourself or anyone else if you keep doing what you're doing.

Truth Verses: Galatians 1:10, Proverbs 16: 2 – 3, 2 Corinthians 9:7

Beautiful Truth

Day 107

Everything you have and are is because of His grace. Nothing is because of your own doing. Today, let go of this arrogant attitude. You're not superior. You're not above the rest. Every good and perfect thing you have comes from the Lord. It's not because you did everything right. It's not because you finished school and had opportunities that others didn't have. It's not because you're so handsome and beautiful, so smart and wise. It's not because of where you came from and the family you have. It's because God's favor is upon you. It's because His grace has been carrying you since you were born. His hand has always been in your life. Recognize that. God's leading and guiding has gotten you to this point. It's been the prayers of your mother, the petitions of your father and the intercessions of others that have kept you from being down and out, from not facing the challenges that others have had to experience. Quit thinking it's because of you. This is how judgment and pride come into your heart. Yes, you're special. But in the eyes of the Lord so is everyone else. We're all one body. He is no respecter of persons. What He does for one, He can and will do for others. Instead of thinking more highly of yourself than you ought, thank Him for His grace. Thank Him for His hand in your life. Thank Him for the blessings you don't even deserve, but that He continues to provide for you. Thank Him for protecting you from things that could've destroyed you. God has been good to you despite your actions. And that's why He deserves the all praise, not you. Remember that.

Truth Verses: Romans 12:3, 1 Corinthians 12:20, 1 Corinthians 12:27, Psalm 106:1

Beautiful Truth

Day 108

If you know better, then why aren't you doing better? There's truly no excuse. Today, learn from your mistakes. God didn't allow you to go through the test and trial for nothing. He didn't allow you to come out of it stronger, wiser and better so you could turn right back around and do the same thing. That's insanity. God saved you so you could save and proclaim His goodness to someone else. He saved you so you can be better and different than you were. Quit thinking you can keep going through life walking around the same mountains, bumping your head against the same walls and it's ok. It's not ok. God has more for you than that. God has created you with a purpose. He has a plan for your life. But if you never learn from the mistakes and bumps in the road, how are you supposed to get to it? How are you supposed to share your testimony, pull others to Christ and change your situation? You're not. You're always going to be right where you are. You're always going to be the person saying "should've, could've, would've." You're always going to be the person living in the past because their present and tomorrow aren't what they want it to be. It all starts with you. Stop blaming the enemy and God for your circumstance. Stop thinking God's against you and is not hearing your prayers. His hearing has nothing to do with your choices. God has given you free will. You don't have to follow or listen to Him. It's your choice to bear, but it's also your consequence. If you want to see the results you're praying for, think more about the action that will lead you to it. You can talk all day about what God isn't doing in your life and what you're still waiting on to happen. But the proof is in the pudding.

**Truth Verses: Matthew 3:8 (NLT), Ephesians 5:8,
Ephesians 5:14 – 16**

Beautiful Truth

Day 109

And does it really matter? The thing you're so concerned about, can you really do anything about it? If not, then why are you stressing about it? Why are you taking on all this worry and panic? Stop it. Today, take it to God. This is not your battle or problem to fix. Jesus came so that you may have and enjoy life, to the full, until it overflows. He didn't endure the cross for you to run around like a chicken with its head cut off. He didn't pay that high price for your life so that you could continue to carry all this weight. He gave up His life so that you may live peacefully and freely. He defeated every pain you could ever have so that you may live pain-free. But do you believe that? Are you truly living it out? Are you living free or are you still walking around with burdens? Release them today. Only Jesus can carry the load you're trying to carry. Don't start doubting Him now. Jesus has been too faithful and good for your doubt. He's been too trustworthy and righteous for you to stop believing Him now. He's the same today as He's always been. He's your Redeemer and good Shepherd. He's your Deliverer. You don't have to be uptight and in a frenzy. God's got you today. Just relax.

Truth Verses: 2 Chronicles 20:15, Isaiah 53: 4 – 5,
Psalm 68:19, John 10:11

Beautiful Truth

Day 110

And yes, it hurt. But at the end of the day, it doesn't matter what somebody has said or did to you. It doesn't matter how wrong or unfair it was. They still have the right to be happy in their life just like you do. Today, stop wishing bad on the ones who hurt you. Sure, what they did caused great pain to you. It wasn't right. But you harboring these bad feelings against them isn't right either. You holding on to the past and what they did years ago, isn't helping you. It's hurting you. Every day you hold on to the offense, you become more bitter. Every day you hold on, you get further away from the blessed life God has for you. You're so busy focusing on what was done to you that you can't see how God is trying to bless you in spite of it. He's moving you through it. He has something greater and better on the other side of it. Let the hurt and offense go. Yes, it's difficult and you'd rather make someone "pay" for what they did to you. But that's not their job. Perhaps they've already paid. You don't know what heartache, misery, and trials they've had to endure because of their actions. Let that be enough. Let God be their judge. You? Let them go. Let them live their life. It's over. Holding on to hurt won't change what's already happened. But letting go will. God loves you so much. He wants to take care of and heal you. Let Him. Then, you can have the wonderful life He's ordained for you to have.

Truth Verses: Matthew 6:12, Ephesians 4:32, James 4:12, Psalm 147:3

Beautiful Truth

Day 111

And you hate waiting. But in this life, you will have to wait. On other people, on things to come to pass, and even on God. Today, get used to it. God will continue to put you in situations where your patience is tested until you learn how to properly wait for His move. Too many times you want to be in control and want things to happen on your time in your way. But God doesn't work like that. He works in steps and in His timing. He has an ultimate plan. And it is good. Wait for it. He's not stalling time or causing you to wait for no reason. He's not trying to torture or drive you crazy. He's building your character. He's building your trust in Him - not in yourself, the situation or the outcome you want. This building shows that you alone have nothing to do with the outcome. It shows your submission to God and that you're more concerned with doing His will than doing your own thing. Stop being upset about waiting. Embrace it. Why? Because you know it's going to work out for your good and His glory regardless of the result. Because you know God has your back. Because you know He is for you, with you and loves you always. This waiting can only be for your very best. Walk in confidence about that. Whether the answer comes now or later, stay confident in the fact that God has your best interest at heart. You know He has you covered. There's no reason to feel like you're losing your mind waiting on Him to lead you. You're not. He's in control of it all. Rest in that today.

Truth Verses: Habakkuk 2:3, Isaiah 25:9, Psalm 103:5

Beautiful Truth

Day 112

And God knows what He's doing. He knows how to provide the very best for you. But you if don't see it like that, you'll never appreciate anything He's doing for you. You'll always think the grass is greener on the other side. Today, your grass is green enough. So many times God is giving you His absolute best, but you still complain. It's not what you think you should have, so you groan and murmur. You're never satisfied. Even when God gives you what you ask for, you still desire more. Learn how to enjoy the blessings God is giving you right now, in this very moment. Be content in all circumstances. God is not misdirected. He knows exactly what to bless you with. He knows what you need even when you don't know it. He can see past any and everything you see. Stop seconding guess this path. It's God's leading and guiding. Contrary to your belief, you're right where you're supposed to be. God hasn't missed a beat with your life and never will. No, it doesn't feel good right now. Yes, you have dreams and visions past this. But you're not there yet. Walk in baby steps. That's how God works - little by little. He's a preparer. He's not going to just throw you into something great and not have you ready for it. He's a patient and loving God. You're not on any timetable. Relax. Trust God right where you are. Trust the God that lives in you. Know that if He wanted you to be somewhere else doing something else, you would be. You may not be "in love" with where you are, but it's for a greater purpose and reason. Find the beauty in it and praise Him for that.

Truth Verses: Numbers 14:2 – 3, 1 Timothy 6:6, 2 Corinthians 9:8

Beautiful Truth

Day 113

And the very thing you're afraid of could be the very thing God is pushing you to do. Today, just because it's the way you've always done it doesn't make it right anymore. The truth is you outgrow people and places. You outgrow relationships and the things that use to bring you pleasure. It's all a part of growing up in God and becoming the person He's called you to be. So when you feel Him tugging at your heart to let some things go, you can't ignore it. You can't act like you don't hear Him. You hear God loud and clear. And you've seen the separation, how He's pulling you away from certain people and things, from certain conversations, from familiar surroundings. You're aware of it. Act like it. Stop sitting there, staying where you are because it's convenient and because you're too scared to try something new. You wouldn't be where you are right now if you would've stayed in the same town, around the same people, in the same job, doing the same thing continuously. It's called progress and forward movement. If you were bold enough to do it before, be bold enough to do it now. Where you are now isn't "it" for you. There are places you haven't even thought of that God wants to show you. There's new people, relationships and resources you haven't even begun to tap into. But you'll never get to any of them staying where you are. Your response and action today determines where you'll be in the future. If God is giving you the green light, go. Don't hold out another moment.

Truth Verses: Genesis 12:1, Isaiah 42:9, 1 Corinthians 2:9

Beautiful Truth

Day 114

And you don't have to accept anything. You don't have to keep eating the "breadcrumbs" of life. Pray about it. Pray about the things you want to change in your life. That's your right through Jesus Christ. That's your authority. Today, if you don't like it, use the power of prayer to change it. The prayers of the righteous are powerful and effective. Don't you know that? Don't you know that's what God has declared about you? You're His righteous. Everything that comes out of you is righteous through Jesus. It doesn't matter what people tell you. It doesn't matter how they label you and what they say isn't so. You have the power of God living down on the inside of you. Wake up. You don't have to keep having these physical aches and pains. Speak to them. Pray for healing. You don't have to keep having long, sleepless nights. Pray for peace. You don't have to keep living pay check to pay check. Pray for wisdom in your finances. Prayer and God are the answer to every problem you have. It's the solution to every issue in your life. No, it's not always the "quick fix" you're looking for. But it's the only thing that will make a real difference in your life. It's the only thing that will work. Quit running to everything else. Run to prayer. Run to God. Why? Because your life is too important and precious to keep putting up with these messy things.

Truth Verses: James 5:16, 1 Corinthians 1:30, Matthew 21:21

Beautiful Truth

Day 115

Did Jesus have to yell, scream, rant and rave to make His point? Did He constantly need to remind people He was the Son of God and the most important? No. Neither should you. Today, nobody can receive anything from you when you're yelling and being aggressive all time. God can't work through you in His power and might when you're full of anger, bitterness, and hatred. That's the root of your aggression. It's bottled up inside of you and you haven't dealt with it. You haven't released it and given it over to God. It's something you're just walking around, living with. But that's not God's best for your life. You don't have to just "live" with anything. Cast your care onto God. Why? Because not only does He care for you, He needs you. He needs you healed and whole so that He can bring His kingdom into this world. But God can't do that with your current attitude. You can't depict Christ with these outbursts. Sure, you may have something worthwhile to say. It may even be helpful. But who wants to hear it when it's coming out as an attack? Soften your approach. You don't have to be rude and rough in your delivery. You don't have to be so hard up. You're just choosing to. Choose to speak and approach people in a different manner. Your attitude and delivery is a choice. It's a conscious effort. Yes, it's hard. But ask God to help you. You have not because you ask not. Ask God to help you speak to others in the way you'd like to be spoken to. Remember, you can kill more bees with honey than vinegar any day.

Truth Verses: Ephesians 4:30 – 31, 1 Peter 5:7, Luke 6:31, Proverbs 16:24

Beautiful Truth

Day 116

Sometimes the answer is right in front of you. You just don't want to admit it. Today, as ugly as it is, don't be afraid to face the truth. Sure, it's not what you want to do. Yes, you are afraid. But where is denying it getting you? How is closing your eyes to the situation or issue helping you? It's not. You're still frustrated, upset and angry. Learn how to face the music. If something isn't working, it's just not working. There's no reason to force change or to wait around, hoping things will be different. If God has shown you the truth, accept it. Ask God what He wants you to do with it. Ask God to show you what's next. It doesn't mean you have to like it. But you do have to start facing the reality of it.

Truth Verses: John 8:32, 3 John 1:4, 1 John 1:6, Psalm 25:5

Beautiful Truth

Day 117

How do you know it won't work when you haven't even attempted to try it? Today, don't knock it yet. You don't know what the outcome is truly going to be. Quit thinking you have it all figured out. You don't. All you know is the fearful suggestions the enemy is throwing your way. All you're focused on is the "what-if" or what could go wrong. But so what if you attempt something and it doesn't turn out like you thought? So what if you step out on faith and it doesn't lead to where you envisioned? What have you truly lost? At least you jumped out there. At least you showed God you trust Him enough to do it. At least you didn't let fear hold you back. Learn how to be ok with that. Everything you do in this life won't always lead to the results you want. It's called life. It's called taking risks. Yes, there are some things that are too risky and costly. Sure, you shouldn't do anything God hasn't given you peace about. But if He's opened up the door and opportunity, why are you just sitting there? Walk through it. That's what faith is all about. It's about reaching for and trying those things you don't and cannot see. Aren't you a person of faith? Aren't you a child of the Most High? Then, act like it. Stop walking around being afraid to take chances, scared of what people will say or how they will react. Jesus took chances. He dared to be different, bold and courageous when others were not. The same goes for you. Learn how to walk like Jesus walked and you'll get the same results He did – victory.

Truth Verses: Isaiah 41:13, Joshua 1:5, Hebrews 11:1

Beautiful Truth

Day 118

And if you think it has the potential to be offensive, it probably is. Today, follow your first mind. The thought of potential offense hasn't come to your mind for no reason. God didn't put it there to just ignore it. It does mean something. It's God warning you, trying to tell you to think before you speak. It's the Holy Spirit intervening, telling you to watch your words. Pay attention. Many relationships are ruined because of words. Somebody didn't use wisdom or discernment before speaking. Someone didn't listen to the Holy Spirit. They didn't allow themselves to be guided by His words and in His truth. You? Be different. Your words are powerful. While it may not be your intentions to hurt or harm someone, you never know how the person will take it. But the Holy Spirit does. That's why He's prompting you. That's why you ask for His guidance before you speak. Quit allowing things to just "fly" out of your mouth. Ask God to direct your words today just like you ask Him to direct everything else.

Truth Verses: Matthew 12:37, Proverbs 13:3, Psalm 19:14

Beautiful Truth

Day 119

Since you've been forgiven much by God, you must return the favor. Today, who do you need to forgive? It doesn't matter if the offense was small or large. It doesn't matter how long ago it happened. What matters is you need to let it go. The offense is holding you back. And if God doesn't continue to hold anything over your head, then why are you holding things over someone else's head? Extend the same mercy and grace to others as God has extended to you. You have no right to keep them in "payment" to you. You have no right to hold them in "bondage" to you. When you do, you keep the offense alive and it will keep affecting you. It will keep holding you back. That's too heavy of a burden for you to bear. If you want to be burden free and walk in true peace, forgive the person. Let the offense go. It's over.

Truth Verses: Colossians 3:13, Proverbs 19:11,
Matthew 5:44, Matthew 11:28 – 30

Beautiful Truth

Day 120

Just because they rejected you doesn't mean there's something wrong with you. The truth is you dodged a bullet. Today, be thankful that it didn't work out. Everything that glitters isn't gold. That's why God said to consult Him in all things. That's why He said to ask and use the Holy Spirit. The Holy Spirit knows all and sees all. He sees behind smiling faces and sweet offerings. He sees beyond people's words and what they're saying. He sees beyond today and the present moment. And He doesn't want you to get hurt. He doesn't want you to get entangled into something that looks good now, but that will break your heart later. He doesn't want you putting your hopes and belief into what seems like the best option now, only to be disappointed and devastated years later. Learn how to trust that. Trust the Holy Spirit in you. God loves you. He's never out to harm or spoil your fun. Nor is He trying to make you suffer. He's trying to lead you to better. Quit being upset about that and the plan that didn't work out. God was protecting and looking out for you. He's leading you to the person and place you've been praying for. But it's not your way or the highway. It's His way. Praise Him for that. Worship Him for that. Be grateful for that. The situation not going your way isn't a loss or setback. It's a setup for something greater and better. Remember that.

Truth Verses: Isaiah 41:9, Psalm 32:7, Ephesians 5:20

Beautiful Truth

Day 121

And you honestly don't know how it's going to turn out. All you have is what you know right now. Today, baby steps. That's how God wants you to walk through this situation. He doesn't need you jumping to conclusions or trying to determine how the ending will be. He needs you to trust Him right now in this very moment, with everything you have. This may not be the path or plan you selected. But God is with you. You're not fighting or standing alone. He has this situation under control, and it's going to work it out for your good and His glory. But in His due time. That's the key to this - God's timing, not yours. He doesn't want you planning ahead or making provisions. Now is not the time for that. Right now is step one, that's the step you're on. Stay there. Quit trying to jump ahead of God. There is a master plan, a method to the madness. But your focus is to stay in the moment and be content in the present, to stay obedient and believe God for His goodness. When it's time for the next step, God will let you know. He knows where and how to find you. Until then, just keep doing what you're doing. Keep honoring Him for what He has, is and will do in your life.

Truth Verses: Isaiah 14:24, Deuteronomy 5:33 (NLT), Isaiah 25:1

Beautiful Truth

Day 122

You're going to get off track from time to time. But God knows where to find you. He knows right where you'll be. Today, be confident in your God, not in yourself or your abilities to put your life back together. You alone can't manage your own life. You can't right your own wrongs or clean up your messes and mistakes. But God can. He knows how to pull you back in and place you right where you got off track. He knows how to shape, form and mold you just like clay. Begin trusting in that. Nobody's saying to go out, make mistakes and get off course on purpose. But when you do, know there's no need to panic. Have peace that God will speak to you and lead you right where you're supposed to be. That's His grace and mercy. Remember that, even if you make a mistake today.

**Truth Verses: Deuteronomy 32:10, Isaiah 64:8,
Lamentations 3:22 – 23**

Beautiful Truth

Day 123

God hasn't left you in the situation because you're weak or unqualified for the next thing. You're in it because you can still handle it. When you can't, He'll be sure to pull you out. Today, you're not sinking, falling or being consumed by it all. Stop speaking and believing that. Your emotions are telling you that. Your family and friends are telling you that. The people around you are telling you that. The truth is if you're still standing and are still here to speak about it, in your right mind and in peace, you're handling it. You're handling every dart the enemy is throwing at you. You're handling every challenge you've faced. You're handling every hard day and long night. You're handling things you don't even understand – every ounce of criticism, every look of disappointment, every accusation, every hurt and pain. You're fighting the good fight, enduring to the end. Sure, you'd rather have it a different way. But this season of not giving up and giving in is all part of the plan. Just because it's not going as you planned doesn't mean you're doing something wrong or that you've missed a step. You haven't. You're right where you need to be. And God is so proud of you. He's proud that you're still standing. Accept the grace and the strength He's given you with honor. All your hard work is not in vain. It's for a greater reward. Remember that.

**Truth Verses: 2 Corinthians 4:8, Isaiah 40:29,
1 Timothy 6:12, 1 Corinthians 15:58**

Beautiful Truth

Day 124

Just because it's hard doesn't mean it's impossible. Today, don't let the difficulty stop you from trying at all. Too many times the minute a situation becomes hard you think it's time to throw in the towel. But you were meant for hard things. You were made to withstand them. Why? Because you have the mind and spirit of Christ within you. There is nothing too hard for God. There is nothing He can't or won't do for you. If He needs to move the mountains and sea, He will. If He needs to place people in the right place at the right time, He will. If He needs to stop time, He will. Why? Because He loves you. But you must believe that. The second you think time, resources, and people are bigger and more important than your God, you lose out. You don't see the victory or His hand in your life. Why? Because you're too focused on what's around you. You're putting too much emphasis on the world and less on God. God is bigger than any problem you face or dream you can imagine. Stop thinking the opposition you're facing is going to shut down the works and power of the Lord. It's not. The opposition is just a part of the process. It's your testimony and way of saying despite the obstacle, God was still able. It's you saying regardless of what tried to come against me, God protected and delivered me. Your opposition is not the problem, or a means to throw in the towel. It's an opportunity for God to show up and show out in your life. Remember that.

Truth Verses: Jeremiah 32:27, Ephesians 3:17 – 20, Exodus 13:9

Beautiful Truth

Day 125

And the question is do you love Jesus more than the person you're begging for Him to change? Do you want the person to change because you truly want what's best for them or do you just want to make your life less complicated? Today, you can't manipulate God into changing someone. It must come from the heart. It must be out of your love for Jesus, not out of your own selfish gain. God isn't interested in making your life easy and comfortable. He's interested in saving souls and bringing people back to Him. Yes, He wants you happy and to enjoy things. But that doesn't mean you get to "tip through the tulips" with people all the time. Sometimes, relationships will just be hard. But it's not your job to make them right or to try to change other people so you can feel better. Your happiness and contentment aren't in them. It's in the Lord. Whether they change or not, your peace, joy, and security should always be in God. You cannot force anyone to change. You can pray for them, but they must be willing to let God transform their heart. That's why your motives have to be pure. You have to want others to change for their own good, not yours. That's what real love and intercession are all about.

**Truth Verses: Luke 19:10, Matthew 9:13, Psalm 51:10,
Proverbs 16:2**

Beautiful Truth

Day 126

The very thing you're complaining about could be the one opportunity you've been searching and praying for. Today, quit seeing the challenge as a burden. It's not. Yes, it's hard and difficult. But right in the midst of it, is a blessing. Right in the midst, God is speaking to you. He's leading and guiding you to His will. Just because it's not coming in the way you thought it would doesn't mean it's wrong. Nor does it mean it's a bad thing or something that isn't meant for you. It is. The best things in life are sometimes disguised in the greatest challenges. Don't allow the challenge to make you think God isn't in it. He is. And He promised to work all things together for your good. That means this too. Instead of seeing it as a problem you can't get rid of, ask God to open your eyes to the possibilities in it. God said He was doing a new thing in your life. And before the new comes, the old must go away. He must pull those old things out of you. That's what's hard and uncomfortable - letting go of the old and how you thought it would be. But God's way is always better. Trust that right now God is leading you to better. This season in your life isn't a curse. It's an eye-opening, jaw-dropping blessing. It may not look like it now. But it will later. Remember that.

Truth Verses: Isaiah 58:11, Mark 2:22, John 15:2, Proverbs 3:5 – 6

Day 127

You're not stuck. There's always a way out, a way of escape. Today, quit saying and thinking you're stuck. You're not stuck in a job, you're not stuck in a relationship, you're not stuck in a career or bad situation. God has already provided the way out. You have options. There's always something you can do. But the question is what's holding you back from doing it? Sure, not every option is the best option. It may not be right or beneficial for you. But it's an option. It's a direction. It's something that can be done about the problem. That's why you're not stuck. God never puts you in situations where you don't have any options. In Him, you have an escape. Start believing that. When you have faith and believe that this situation isn't your last hope or final destination, it empowers you. It gives you the strength you need to go forward. It provides you with the confidence and willpower to seek God's ways and paths. It gives you the trust and courage to be bold and not only call those things that be not as they are, but to pursue them. Begin living your life like this. Contrary to your belief, regardless of what you've heard or seen others do, God didn't create you to be miserable and to just "endure" terrible situations all your life. He has more for you than that. Just like He sent Moses to free the Israelites, your Moses is coming too. Your due season of deliverance is here. Receive it and be on the lookout for it.

Truth Verses: 1 Corinthians 10:13, Psalm 16:11, Romans 4:17, Exodus 3:7 – 10

Beautiful Truth

Day 128

You don't have to "chase" after anything. If it's yours, it's yours. It's not going anywhere. Nothing and nobody can take it away from you. Today, be confident in the things God has declared for you. You don't have to be timid or afraid. You don't have to please and stay in people's good graces to keep it. People didn't give you what you have. The Lord provided it to you. Every blessing, provision, and good and perfect gift is from above. It was the Lord's hand on your life. It was the Lord's hand that put this blessing together for you. He connected the right people at the right time for you. He softened their heart towards you. It wasn't who you knew, how smart you were or how many degrees you had. God's favor was upon you. That's why you're successful and blessed. Stop forgetting that. When you chase behind people and beg them to accept or choose you so you can maintain a certain lifestyle or sense of belonging, you're wrong. You're honoring them above God. You're trusting and believing in their resources more than you're trusting and believing in God. Stop it. You're a child of God. Put your trust and faith in Him alone. He's Alpha and Omega, beginning and the end. He's a jealous God and shouldn't have to compete with others in your life. Keep the Lord in His proper place. Keep Him first. Whatever He's blessed you with, He's going to be the One to help you keep it. He doesn't "giveth" and "taketh" away. If you stay close to the vine and in His presence, He's going to tell you what to do, how to do it and when. You won't have the risk of losing anything because you'll be in His wise counsel and safe arms.

Truth Verses: James 1:17, Genesis 39:2, Deuteronomy 4:24, John 15:5

Day 129

And what do you do when you've been waiting for so long? Keep waiting until the change comes. Today, the length of time means nothing to God. What seems like a thousand years to you is merely seconds in His eyes. He's not sitting there tracking how long you've praying about something. He's not standing there counting the years you've been in the same situation. Yes, it's frustrating. No, He doesn't want to see you in agony. But God's timing is perfect. He never provides too early or too late. He knows exactly what to give you when. You may feel like you're on your last leg, like you can't take another moment of your situation. But you can. You're tougher than you think. You're stronger than what you give yourself credit for. You could've given up by now. You could've thrown in the towel and turned your back on God and His promises. But you haven't. You've waited patiently for His leading and guiding. You didn't follow the crowd or just do what you wanted to do. You've been angry and frustrated, but you haven't quit. You haven't abandoned God and what you believe. Let that count for something. Let that be a victory for you. God will reward you for your efforts. Your work is not in vain. He is going to deliver and come through for you. That's a promise.

**Truth Verses: 2 Peter 3:8 – 9, Revelation 2:3,
Psalm 126:5, Hebrews 6:13 –15**

Beautiful Truth

Day 130

If you want a different outcome, make a different decision. It's that simple. Today, stop doing the same thing and expecting a different result. That's insanity. Certain actions bring certain consequences and results…period. You can pray about it. You can ask God to remove people and things from your life, but until you make up your mind to change the decisions you're making, nothing will change. The same bad result you're getting now, you'll continue to get. It's not God or the enemy's fault. It's self-deception. See the truth about yourself today. While God hasn't called you to walk in condemnation or guilt about your decisions, He also hasn't called you to be in denial. He hasn't called you to walk around with blinders on, blaming everyone else for your problems. Some of the things you're going through are from your own unwise choices. Some of the wounds and pain you're feeling are self-inflicted. Yes, there's grace for the things you've done. Yes, God will still cover and keep you. But you will only get so far in life with those poor habits. God can't unleash and unlock His promises when you have poor decision making. Why? Because your character isn't developed. You're not showing any sign that your character can handle more blessings. You're not walking in the fruit of the spirit. You're walking in the flesh. God knows you're trying, but He wants you to do better than just "trying." He wants you to put your best foot forward. He wants you to think through your decisions before you make them. It's hard to resist temptation, but lean on God for strength. You don't have to resist alone. Open your mouth and ask God to give you more wisdom in the areas you need it. You have not because you ask not. But when you humble yourself and ask God for help, you'll begin to see changes in your decisions.

Truth Verses: Proverbs 3:7, Galatians 5:19 – 22, 1 Kings 3:12

Beautiful Truth

Day 131

If it's supposed to happen, it will. Nothing and no one can change that. Today, stop worrying about it. Your worrying isn't making the situation any better. Nor is it changing the result. The outcome is the outcome. You can beg, plead and pray about it all you want. But if it's not good enough for you, God will not give it to you...period. As much as you want this thing to work out in your favor, God knows what's best. This route, the one you think is so right, may not be right for you at all. There may be something behind it that is dangerous, something you can't see that will hurt or harm you. But all you see right now is what you want. And all you want is deliverance in this very moment. God knows and understands that. But He also sees all sides of the whole situation. And if He's saying "no" to something in your life, there's a reason for it. Whether it's a relationship, a job change, a move, or a large purchase, trust God's "no" today. Be confident that He's trying to look out for you and make your life better, not worse. You don't have to necessarily like it, but stop thinking God's out to hurt you. Yes, His "no" hurts. But it could hurt a lot worse later if He says "yes" right now. Remember that.

Truth Verses: Isaiah 48:3, Psalm 84:11, Psalm 91:10

Beautiful Truth

Day 132

Just because it's buried doesn't mean it's not there. It's still there. You know it and God knows it. Today, it's still an issue. Yes, you prayed about it and begged God to take the pain away. But you still feel the same way you felt before. That issue, problem, or thing you can't seem to shake, is still plaguing you. Why? Because you haven't properly dealt with it. Overlooking it isn't dealing with it. Avoiding it isn't dealing with it. Just trying not to talk about it isn't dealing with it. When God reveals an issue to you, He wants you to acknowledge it. He didn't show it to you for you to run away. He didn't bring it up so you wouldn't have to address it. God wants you to deal with it. Why? Because He wants you whole. He knows this issue is holding you back. He knows it's kept you down and out. He knows it's caused you to miss opportunities and blessings. God knows it stirs up fear and anxiety. And He wants better for you. Let Him provide it to you. Quit thinking you have the answers or that you don't have to deal with things. You do. But the good thing is you don't have to deal with them alone. God is here to help you. How? Through His healing. Allow Him to mend your broken heart. Allow Him to heal and restore all the hurt and pain you feel. God is your answer in all of this. He is with you and wants you well. But you must let Him work in your life. You must let Him work this issue and hurt out of you. It's the only way you'll be free and get to victory. Remember that.

Truth Verses: Jeremiah 17:14, 3 John 1:2, Jeremiah 33:6

Beautiful Truth

Day 133

Just because people didn't support you doesn't mean you do the same to others. Today, be the help you didn't get. Yes, you feel hurt and rejected. You feel abandoned, like you had nobody in your corner. But that's not true. You have never done anything alone. God has always been in your corner. He has always been right by your side, cheering you on, leading you step by step. And because He's been here for you, you need to be here for somebody else. Being unsupportive and cold-hearted isn't being a blessing. It's not being a light and vessel in this dark world. It isn't being the salt of the earth. It's making you bitter and causing others to be stagnant. You're holding up their progress and blessings. How? Because their movement is tied to yours. Their progress is tied to what you're supposed to provide to them. Quit holding others up because you're not healed from how you were treated. Go to God. Open your mouth and be honest before Him. Tell Him how upset and angry you are about what you didn't receive from others. Tell Him the truth so that you may be free and healed from your past. You'll never get where you need to be until you get rid of the bitterness and resentment in your heart. Give and it shall be given unto you. Give the very thing you wanted but didn't receive. That's how you become a blessing to others and in God's kingdom.

Truth Verses: Isaiah 60:1 – 2, Matthew 5:13 – 16, John 8:32, Luke 6:38

Beautiful Truth

Day 134

And just because you overheard or seen it doesn't mean you need to gossip about it. It is not your job to go talking about what has happened in someone else's life. Today, keep things to yourself. Is someone hurt? Are they in danger? Is it a true emergency? If not, why are you discussing it with someone else? What value or benefit is it bringing to you except to make you feel like you're a leader of something? The truth is every negative thing you hear or see isn't meant to be told to the next person. It's gossip. And it's how you become untrustworthy. It's how you get into backbiting and judgment. Every day you will be tested in this area. God will put you in certain places at certain times to see how you will react and if you'll cover someone's flaws with love or if you'll expose them. He'll see if you can really be the salt and light you're claiming to be. The truth is people who are truly salt change their atmosphere and environment. They don't adapt to it. They don't act and sound like everyone else around them. They don't do the same things others do. They're different. So the question is how different are you? Are you different from the very environment you're complaining about? Are you adding to or taking away from it? Are you the one people are running to or away from in your circle, on your job, at your church, in your community? People want to be around someone who is uplifting and encouraging. Be above the gossip and negativity today. Walk in the image of Christ. Act how He would act. Would He go around telling other people's business and spreading what happened to them? No. The same goes for you. Be the answer to this hurting world, not another problem in it.

Truth Verses: 1 Timothy 5:13, Psalm 101:5, Psalm 15:1 – 3, 1 Peter 2:1

Beautiful Truth

Day 135

Even in your worse situation, you could be considered better off than someone else. Today, remember that. As hard as it is, be thankful for what you do have. So many times you look at your situation through clouded lenses. All you see is what you're lacking and what God hasn't delivered on yet. And while you do still have needs, you've also been greatly taken care of. God has covered you. Not a hair on your head has been touched. Not a moment has God failed, left or forsaken you. Sure, you may not have gotten what you wanted, but God hasn't left you out in the cold. He hasn't left you out there on your own. He's made a way for you. Be grateful for that. Be grateful for the good and bad days. God doesn't want you looking at the circumstance and determining if you're going to be thankful. God wants you thankful at all times. Why? Because thankfulness puts the focus on Him, not on you or the problem. Walk in gratitude about your life. Nobody's saying you need to like the situation. God knows you don't want to be in it. But He's giving you the grace to go through it. He's giving you the strength to keep moving forward and the faith to believe. And for that, you should be grateful. It's not about getting your problem resolved. It's about keeping focused and receiving His love through it.

**Truth Verses: Nehemiah 9:18 – 21, Philippians 4:4,
1 Chronicles 16:11**

Beautiful Truth

Day 136

It's hard to love someone else and see the good in them when you don't love and see the good in yourself. Today, until you change your perspective of yourself, you'll always have a problem with other people. They'll never treat you fair enough. They'll never be loyal enough. They'll never be worthy enough, kind enough or caring enough to fit your needs. Nothing will ever be enough. No matter how hard they try to stay in your good graces, you'll always find something wrong. But the truth is they're not the problem. Your perspective and outlook on life is. You're so busy looking at the world through negativity and disappointment that it's all you see. And it's hurting you. It's destroying your relationships. Can't you see that? Contrary to your belief, there is not something wrong with everyone you meet. You're being deceived by your own thoughts. Open your eyes to the truth today. Yes, people have hurt and treated you wrong. Sure, bad things have happened. But everyone is not to blame. It's not the whole world's fault. Quit generalizing everyone for one person's mistake. What you truly need is to be healed from your past, from those old wounds. Then, and only then will you begin to love yourself as Christ does and see others in the same way.

Truth Verses: Mark 12:31, Psalm 147:3, Isaiah 35:5

Beautiful Truth

Day 137

And what other people are or aren't doing isn't your battle. It's God. Today, quit running around talking about what others are doing to you. Take the concern up with God. The truth is nobody can truly do anything about the problem except God. Yes, it's good to vent and to get things off your chest. But what is the plan to resolve the issue once you're done complaining about it? What do you have left? Nothing, but anger and frustration. Stop going around the same mountain. Tell your feelings to God. Contrary to your belief, God knows everything you know and even more about the situation. He sees what people are doing to you and around you. He knows if they're right or wrong. But He will continue to let you stay in the mess you're in until you ask for His help. He'll continue to let you grovel and complain, and stress yourself out until you decide to reach out to Him. God is your help and refuge in all things. Stop forgetting that. Stop picking and choosing what He should be included in. This is why you complain, but never seem to find a solution to your problems. Ask God to dwell in the midst of your issues before you go off and start speaking and dealing with things on your own. God knows your frustrations with certain people. And He'll either change you, change them or change the situation. Regardless, the answer isn't the way you're dealing with them right now. As hard as it, strive to keep your mouth closed about others. Instead, open your mouth to God in prayer about these concerns. That's how you truly combat these frustrations with others.

Truth Verses: 1 Corinthians 10:10, Psalm 34:4, Psalm 141:3

Beautiful Truth

Day 138

And every temptation starts with a thought. If you think about it and see yourself engaged in it long enough, you're going to do it. Before long, you're going to carry out the very thing you've been tempted with. Today, be careful of your wandering thoughts. Everything that comes to your mind isn't from God. Every thought you have about the past, present or future isn't of the Lord. God never comes to tempt you. That's the enemy. He's the one who wants to get you off the path. He's the one who leads you to believe the thought in your mind is so much better than your reality. He wants you to believe you're missing out on something. But you're not. It's a trick. Don't fall for it. God supplies everything you need. If you honestly need it, don't you know you'll have it in due time? Don't you know God will freely give to you? Then, act like it. Walk in your power and authority. Cast down these wrong, tempting thoughts. How? Ask God to give you His thoughts. The minute temptation comes into your head, don't let it linger. Don't just try to think about something else. On purpose and out loud, tell the thought to leave your mind in Jesus' name. Then, ask the Lord to cover your mind with His precious blood. Ask Him to give you His words and scriptures to meditate on. That's how you combat the wiles and tricks of the enemy. You don't just sit there and accept it. You use the word of the God to resist the thought. The enemy has no real power over you. He only has suggestions, a "bark." He will only bite if you invite him to. Remember that.

**Truth Verses: James 1:13, Philippians 4:8,
Romans 8:32, 2 Corinthians 10: 4 – 5**

Beautiful Truth

Day 139

God has called for you to help, not to judge and criticize people who are in need. Today, you're blessed to be a blessing - not a curse and barrier to people. You're supposed to be helping, not hurting. The reason why you've become so frustrated and irritated with others is because you're too busy judging what they're doing instead of carrying out the task they need help with. Nobody asked you to determine if they have the discipline or willpower to do the things God has called them to do. Nobody asked you to comment on and tell the world their flaws. Nobody asked you to give your opinion on whether they're doing the right or wrong thing. What did God tell you to provide? Was it peace? Was it love, joy, support or money? A listening ear? Are you doing any of it? Quit prying into other people's lives, trying to be their counselor or psychologist. Focus on what God instructed you to do. If someone needs you to analyze them, they'll ask you. Otherwise, only provide what's asked of you. If it's support, then support them. If it's encouragement, then encourage them. Yes, it's important to know who you're giving your time and resources to. But once you've decided to help someone, you can't gossip and talk about them. You decided to be a part of their lives and to help them, so do just that. Don't be the person that's supportive in their face, but talking negatively about them behind their back. That's not friendship, loyalty or trust. It's backbiting. If you can't completely be on someone's side, remove yourself from the relationship. Period.

Truth Verses: Romans 2:1, Proverbs 17:9, Matthew 7:12

Beautiful Truth

Day 140

And it's ok to be happy. It's ok to have the joy of the Lord. Today, just because you're used to bad doesn't mean it's right. God never intended for you to live an unhappy life. It was never His will for you to feel down and out, depressed and disgusted about your life. Jesus died for you to live, and to live life to the full. You shouldn't walk around feeling bad about your life. You shouldn't look around, waiting for the other shoe to drop. You shouldn't think you're never going to get out of this. You are. You will overcome. This season and situation is temporary. It's not your final destination. It's not the final chapter or story of your life. Quit believing that. The enemy has tricked you and made you think "bad" is all you're going to get. And if you continue to believe his lies and think in this way, that's all you will have and see. Your thoughts dictate your actions and what you'll have in this life. If you truly want the promises of God and to experience His joy, choose to think differently. Choose to expect good things to happen to you at all times. God is your good Shepherd. You're the righteousness of God in Christ and you have a blood-bought right to His goodness. It's a promise from God. Remember that.

Truth Verses: Nehemiah 8:10, John 10:10, Psalm 112:7, Psalm 23:6

Beautiful Truth

Day 141

You're so focused on the bad things about yourself. But what about the good? Today, learn how to see the good in yourself. Concentrate on what you do well. Concentrate on why people love and care for you so much. The enemy works overtime to show you how bad you're messing up all the time. He works around the clock to point out the negative things people say about you. He never reminds you of how much people appreciate you. He never recalls how many times you've made a difference in other people's lives. He never brings up all the gestures and extra things you do for others out of the kindness of your heart. He never shows you how great you truly are. But God does. He sees it. And that's what He chooses to focus on. That's what He sees when He looks and thinks of you. He never sees your wrongs. Why? Because all your wrongs have been forgotten and forgiven through Jesus. When He sees you, He sees His perfect Son. He sees Jesus' righteousness. He sees the ultimate sacrifice that was made on the cross. And on that cross, your sins were laid down and put to rest forever. Put them to rest in your own life too. Quit allowing your past, present, and even future sins to haunt you. It's over. You're a new creature in Christ. Old things have passed away. This is who you are now. Everything you do is all good through Jesus your Savior. Keep your heart and mind focused on that instead of your flaws. Then, the enemy will flee from you and stay in his rightful place.

**Truth Verses: 1 Samuel 16:7, Hebrews 10:17,
Romans 3:24, 2 Corinthians 5:17**

Beautiful Truth

Day 142

And as much as you plan, sometimes life just happens. And when it does, you must trust God and go with the cards you've been dealt. Today, it's ok. No, you didn't think or plan for it to go this way. But God did. He knew this was in the cards and the plan. And although this looks like a setback, it's not. God never intended for this issue, financial hardship, relationship or change to destroy you. Yes, it's something He's allowing to happen, but you were created to overcome it. It's not supposed to crush you. It's not supposed to be a permanent thing in your life. Quit allowing these temporary and minor challenges to become constant battles in your life. How? Go into them knowing you're coming out greater on the other side. That's the key to not being held down or back by life. Sure, you know things don't always go your way. But when they don't, you don't allow them to become the "new normal." Keep pushing forward no matter how hard it is. Grab hold of Jesus, and let Him lead you, day by day, step by step. Stay closer than you've ever been to His presence. Rely on Him solely, not on your smarts, wits, or the advice of your family and friends. God is your refuge, the key to getting over this problem. Don't let this issue overtake you right now. Yes, it's very hard and scary. It may be the hardest thing you've experienced in life. But this is not how your life will always be. This is not "it" for you. Walk with God and push through to the other side.

Truth Verses: Psalm 33:11, 2 Corinthians 4:17 – 18, James 4:8, Philippians 3:13 – 14

Beautiful Truth

Day 143

There will always be someone who will bring out the worst in you, that being around them for too long will make you say or do things that aren't pleasing to God. Today, stay away from those people. There's no going around them sometimes or for a little awhile. There's no "waiting for them to change." You've already been waiting for them to change. You've already been asking and interceding on their behalf for years. You've believed and kept believing. You've fasted and prayed. And yes, God can change them. He can save them just like He did you. But that still doesn't change the fact that right now being around them hurts you. It doesn't help you. It brings you down instead of up. It takes you back instead of forward. They simply bring no value to you at this point in their life. Your soul and spirit simply can't handle them. Your character can't endure them. And you can't afford to get wrapped back up in the wrong lifestyle, doing the wrong things again. You've worked too hard to get to where you are. God saved you from the darkness for a reason. He pulled you out of it for a reason. Remain out of it.

**Truth Verses: Job 16:20 – 21, Proverbs 18:24,
Proverbs 12:26, Proverbs 13:20**

Beautiful Truth

Day 144

And it's because you think you know so much that you're in the situation you're in now. Today, you don't have this life all figured out. Recognize that. It's your pride that's causing you to bump your head against the wall. It's your stubbornness that's allowing you to keep going around the same mountain. It's your control of things that's causing you to shut the very people and things out that God is trying to bless you with. You keep asking God for change. You keep asking God for better. But you're the hold up. It's not God or the enemy. It's your lack of openness. It's your "know-it-all" attitude. But you don't know it all. And that's ok. You have the Lord. Learn to rely on Him. Lean on Him. You don't have to be the smartest person in the room. You don't have to be the wisest one, always knowing what to do. You know God. Go to Him. Instead of being prideful and relying on yourself, ask your Savior. He has every answer you need. He knows it all. Be open to His spirit and leading. Be receptive to His knowledge. Then, you'll get to everything else you need.

Truth Verses: Proverbs 16:18, Proverbs 11:2, Jeremiah 9:23 – 24

Beautiful Truth

Day 145

And when God assigns you to do something you don't understand, you'll feel foolish. But that doesn't mean you are. Today, take your feelings out of it. What God has you doing right now makes no sense. But what does it "making sense" have to do with anything? How is that relevant for carrying out the tasks of the Lord? It's not. If you've chosen to follow His will and plans for your life, then this is it. This is what you signed up for. It doesn't matter how foolish or unwise you appear to others. It doesn't matter how many times the enemy says you're ignorant for what you're doing. It's a lie. You're a wise and intelligent person. You're a child of God who follows the Lord. There's no foolishness in that. Quit letting the enemy deceive you. Yes, you're entitled to how you feel. But you're not your feelings. Who you are at the core is something totally different. You're obedient to God. You know His voice and you follow it. And if God has told you to embark on this path and you have peace about it, then that's all there is to it. Stop listening to the enemy and others. Follow the peace God has given you. Follow His leading. When you do, you'll discover the answers and directions you've been looking for all along.

Truth Verses: 1 Corinthians 1:27, Isaiah 48:17, Colossians 3:15

Beautiful Truth

Day 146

And what are you believing in Jesus for if you don't think He can really help you? Why are you saying He "can do all things" if you never really use His power when you need it? Today, either Jesus is your refuge and fortress in all situations or He isn't. Too many times you call on Jesus in certain circumstances, but not in all circumstances. Why? Because you think you can handle it. You think you only need to call upon Him when circumstances get out of control and over your head. But the truth is every problem you face is over your head. Every issue you encounter is too much for you. This is why you need your Savior. Whether it's money or guidance on how to deal with difficult people, Jesus cares. He cares about everything you do. He cares about you being upset and hurt. He cares about you being worried. He cares about any and everything that impacts your life. Jesus wants to be a part of it all. You don't have to go through life figuring things out on your own. You don't have to go through life, pitiful, not having what you need. You have Jesus. Use Him. Use His name. Use His authority. Reach out to Him. Quit letting these circumstances overwhelm you. Talk to Jesus about them just like you would talk to anybody else. Tell Him what's going on and how you feel. He is on your side. All you have to do is ask for His help and He'll provide everything you need. Remember that.

Truth Verses: Psalm 91:2, Isaiah 41:10, John 14:12, Matthew 7:7

Beautiful Truth

Day 147

And no, you're not a failure. God hasn't put you on a shelf and just left you there. He's preparing you. Today, what feels like a denial is just a wait. God hasn't allowed for you to go through everything you're going through for no reason. All your hard work, blood, sweat, and tears, isn't for not. There's a reason and a purpose for the pain. No, you can't understand it right now. But you're not supposed to. This is your process and journey to the next step. You don't have to understand it. You just have to get through it. You just have to get to the end, to the other side. The only sight you need to keep in mind right now is the Lord's. It's not about you knowing why or when. You have to trust that where you are is right where you're supposed to be. Then, you must be content in it. You can't be ok with it one day and upset about it the next. That's not true contentment. Real contentment is having joy and peace in the circumstance regardless of how bad it is or how bad it gets. Why? Because you trust God. And you know He's not going to let you sink or fall. He's either going to change the situation or deliver you from it. So stop worrying and wondering. Either way, deliverance is coming. Just ask God to give you the grace and endurance to get to it.

Truth Verses: Psalm 27:14, Philippians 4:11,
2 Corinthians 12:9, Psalm 50:15

Beautiful Truth

Day 148

Just because it looks "doom and gloom" doesn't mean it is. God is still able. Today, don't discredit your Lord. Don't you know the God you serve? Have you forgotten how powerful and mighty He is? Have you forgotten how much He loves and adores you? He would move the mountains and the sea for you. He would go to the ends of the earth to find and protect you, to keep you under His wings. Look at what He did for the Israelites. Look how faithful and true He was to them. You're no different. The same type of love and passion He had for them, He has for you. God is always thinking of you, always wanting to bless and care for you. Quit letting the situation make you think differently. Just because you don't see movement in the direction you want doesn't mean there isn't any movement at all. God is moving in His perfect direction and His perfect time. If He's gotten you this far in life, He'll get you through this season of difficulty as well. Yes, you don't know how much more you can take. But you don't have to "take" anything. Give these burdens over to God completely. Have you done all you can, all you know how? Then stand. And keep standing. That's what the Word says and what God has instructed you to do. You don't have to walk around with fear and doubt, thinking things are not going to work out. They are going to work out. Pick yourself up and dust yourself off. Put a smile on your face. God's working on your behalf today and every day. You have nothing to be concerned about.

Truth Verses: Deuteronomy 7:8 – 9, Numbers 6:24,
1 Peter 5:7, Ephesians 6:13

Beautiful Truth

Day 149

And desperate times don't call for desperate measures. You can be patient. You can wait on God. Today, slow down. Just because you think it's a crisis doesn't mean that it is. Don't you know God's in control? Don't you know He has a plan for every situation that comes about, including this one? Then, act like it. Trust Him enough to wait on His guidance. Trust Him enough to open the right doors for you. You don't have to open doors for yourself. God said He opens what no man can close. He said no height, length, or depth can separate or keep Him from you. If He said it, then believe it. Believe that He loves you enough to take care of everything that concerns you, including this situation. He knows how much you're hurting. He knows how hard and tough this is. And you don't have to figure it out or get the answer on your own. Learn how to wait on Him to provide it. You're not supposed to be figuring out what to do in an anxious or desperate attempt. Rest. It's going to be ok. The grace of God is here to help you, to open the windows of heaven and pour out blessings. All you need to do sit back and receive them. Remember that.

**Truth Verses: Isaiah 40:31, Psalm 20:7, Revelation 3:8,
Romans 8:39, Malachi 3:10**

Beautiful Truth

Day 150

And when it's right, it's right. You don't have to force it. It just flows together. Today, quit trying to make things work that you know aren't right. Something in your heart is giving you hesitation. Something in your mind is telling you it shouldn't be this difficult, this taxing, this uncomfortable. Something is telling you this just isn't it. Follow that voice. It's not just "something" in your head. It's the Holy Spirit. It's Christ that lives in you. It's Him leading and guiding you. Isn't that what you've been praying and asking for? Then, follow His leading. Just because He's not guiding you to this one thing doesn't mean He's not guiding you at all. He is. He's leading you right to where you need to be. He's eliminating every wrong choice so that you can make the right one without doubt and regret. He's cutting out every wrong path so you can be sure of the best path. You don't have to "try" to make anything just work. God is the creator of all things. What's for you is not only yours, but it will bring you abundant peace. Wait for that peaceful path. Wait for the peaceful solution, the one that brings you ease. If you have any ounce of wavering or doubt, perhaps that's the Holy Spirit trying to tell you something. Perhaps that's just not the right path for you. Remember that today.

Truth Verses: John 16:13, Proverbs 1:33, 2 Thessalonians 3:16

Beautiful Truth

Day 151

And if it's not one thing, it's another. That's life. But that's also a reminder that you need God. Today, quit looking for the perfect setup. It doesn't exist. Quit looking for the perfect day. That doesn't exist either. Your disappointment with life is your expectation from it. It's not God tricking you, it's not the enemy attacking you. It's your own thoughts. If you think that just because God delivered you from one situation that another problem or issue won't or shouldn't come up, you're wrong. You're deceiving yourself. Something else will always come up. But that doesn't mean you walk around with worry and fear, waiting for the other shoe to drop. That doesn't mean you sit on edge expecting it. You get up each day expecting His goodness. And even when things don't go your way, when the unexpected comes up, you still look to God's goodness. You recognize that He's still for you, with you and loves you. You recognize that the weapon may come, but it's not prospering. You recognize that whatever "it" is, you can handle it because Christ is in you. That's how you live this life. That's how you remain successful. Quit walking around in a fantasy, being devastated when trials and tests come your way. Yes, things are hard, even tragic at times. But after you wipe your tears and get your emotions in control, know that God is still on top of the situation. Weeping may endure for a night, but joy comes in the morning. You've already won the victory. Remember that as you face encounters today.

**Truth Verses: Psalm 27:13, Psalm 30:5,
Colossians 1:27, 1 Corinthians 15:57**

Beautiful Truth

Day 152

You may want to feel sorry for yourself and wallow in self-pity. But you really can't. Why? Because deep in your heart, you know God's got you. You know He's got this. Today, He said He would never leave nor forsake you. And He means it. It's not a lie or something to just hold you over. It's not just words to make you feel better. When God speaks, He means it. When He promises, He delivers. God is not like other people. He's not selling you a dream. He's with you in this life. He's with you through the sun, storm, and rain. Quit believing you're out here on your own or that you're forgotten. That's a lie the enemy tells you so you can keep feeling sorry for yourself. Stop it. Trust God at all times. Just because it's hard right now doesn't mean it's ok for you to doubt Him. It's in this hard place that you need to trust and believe Him even more. No matter how ugly, confusing and painful your situation looks, God's not leaving you down and out in it. He's delivering you right now in this very minute. Stop dwelling on the problem and how bad you feel about it. Dwell on Him and how faithful He is. This whole thing is going to work out better than what you think. You haven't seen anything yet. The best is yet to come.

Truth Verses: Hebrews 6:18, Joshua 1:5, Psalm 62:8

Beautiful Truth

Day 153

And everyone must find their own way, including your kids, spouse, and friends. It's not your job to figure out what they should be doing and how. Only God can do that. Your job? Pray and keep praying. Today, you can't force people to change. You can't force them to do what you want them to do. This is their life. These are their choices and decisions. Just like you had to figure out your life and what to do in it, so do they. Yes, you love them and only want what's best for them. But how often did you listen to advice? How often did you want to do your own thing and discover it in your own way? The same goes for them. They must learn certain things for themselves. As much as you want to hold the hands of the ones you love, you can't. You can't walk or talk for them, so you can't change their behavior either. Learn how to give them over to God completely. Take your hands off the situation. It's not your battle to fight or your problem to fix. This is a God thing. It's God that lives and breathes in people. It's Him that plants, waters and makes things grow. It's Him that changes hearts, not you. Put your prayers where your actions are. Quit nagging and criticizing others, telling them how much they need to change. Love on them instead. Pray and intercede for them. Take your petitions and feelings to God. Tell Him how you feel. Ask Him to do a mighty work in their lives. The power of your prayers gives life. It's what changes things, not your complaints and judgments.

Truth Verses: Ephesians 1:15 –18, 1 Timothy 2:1,
Ephesians 6:18, James 5:16

Beautiful Truth

Day 154

And you've done all you can do. Now? You trust and believe. You leave it in God's hands. Today, that's your one and only role. It's not to keep thinking about it. It's not to keep wondering and worrying about it. It's not to talk negative about it or walk in fear. It's to step aside, and to put and keep your attention on God. You prayed about it and told God how you felt. Why isn't that enough? Why does it need to be anything more added to it? It doesn't. He heard you. He knows what's going on. He knows what you need and how to supply it. Let Him. Let Him bring this thing to pass for you. What's yours is yours...period. You don't have to compete, fight, beg, steal or borrow for it. The devil can't change what's rightfully yours. Neither can people or things. Worrying about it doesn't change the outcome. It just shows that you're not trusting the Lord. Show God you know how to trust in Him with all your heart today. Walk away from the issue. Leave it alone. Leave it in His hands and be at rest.

Truth Verses: Psalm 56:3, Luke 12:25 – 26, Exodus 33:14

Beautiful Truth

Day 155

And no, every person isn't like that. That's just who you know. Today, don't let one bad apple spoil the whole bunch. Don't let one bad experience cause you to generalize and settle for just "anything." You're the righteousness of God in Christ. You're a child of God, precious in His sight. The head, not the tail. He wants you honored and respected in all areas of your life. He wants you loved and cherished in every scenario. He wants you to know who you are, that you deserve the best always. God has not called you to just "settle" for anything. That's the enemy saying you aren't good enough. That's him bringing up your past, throwing it back up in your face. Stop listening to it. God has more for you than what you're allowing. He has more for you than what you're calling "the best" or "doing well." He has more for you than what you see. God has greatness in store for you in your relationships with other people. Quit thinking this situation is the best you can get. Don't you know you serve a mighty God? Don't you know He's able to do exceedingly, abundantly, above all you can ask for or imagine? Don't you know there's nothing He won't do for you? Try Him. Test Him out. And see if He would not open the windows of Heaven for you.

**Truth Verses: Deuteronomy 28:13, Ephesians 3:20,
2 Corinthians 9:8, 1 Corinthians 2:9**

Beautiful Truth

Day 156

People will give you a hundred reasons why you're going through what you're going through, why what you did or prayed for didn't work. But the truth is they have no clue. Nobody really knows why but the Lord. Today, stop listening to people and their theories. Are they God? Are they the ruler of heaven and earth? Do they truly know why things have and haven't happened for you? No. They're just speculating. Yes, their intentions may be good and they just want to help. But your real help comes from the Lord. Only He knows why the situation didn't turn out how you wanted it to. Only He knows the plan, how it all fits together and what's coming next. He knows it all. Start consulting with Him instead of other people. Quit allowing them to fill your head with their opinions. Ask God what went wrong in the situation. Ask God why He didn't allow this particular thing in your life. Ask Him if it's something you need to see or hear differently. Ask Him what you need to do. If you ask, you will receive. God will tell you according to His will. He'll lead and guide you. Then, you'll know for sure what's going on and you won't have to be in confusion. You can walk in peace, the peace God always intended for you to have. Remember that.

**Truth Verses: Leviticus 19:31, Matthew 7:7,
2 Corinthians 3:16, Isaiah 26:3**

Beautiful Truth

Day 157

And that's the problem: you think you don't have to fight for anything in this life. You feel like it should be given to you because you choose to serve God. But you're wrong. Today, the promises of God will not be handed to you. You must fight to possess and obtain them. Contrary to your belief, the enemy's reputation is on the line just like God's. He will not allow you to just obtain the things of God because you pray and go to church, or because you know a few scriptures. The enemy's job is to bring opposition to God's promises. He has a plan just like God does. He doesn't want to see you happy, whole and well. He doesn't want to see you successful in your marriage. He doesn't want you prospering in your job. He doesn't want you walking in divine health. The enemy wants you to suffer. He wants you to back down, give up and stop trying. But you must learn to beat him at his own game. How? Stay the course. Keep at it. Yes, you're in a battle and a fight. But the fight is fixed. You win. You win in all things at all times. The devil is already defeated. He is already the loser in this. You're already on victory's ground. Stop looking at your feelings. Look to God. Look at His character. Is He a liar? Would He promise you something and not deliver? No. Then, you have no reason to doubt Him. Yes, you're tired of fighting. But those who hope in the Lord will be strengthened and renewed. Ask God for grace and endurance in this race. The enemy will not win this round or any other round of your life. You're victorious, more than a conqueror. A survivor, an overcomer. Fight like it today.

Truth Verses: Colossians 2:15, Numbers 23:19, Isaiah 40:31

Beautiful Truth

Day 158

Contrary to your belief, you need this challenge. You need to get out of your comfort zone. Today, the challenge you're running from is the very one working in your favor. How? It's teaching you to be the very person God has called you to be. It's stretching you in ways you can't imagine. It's developing you like nothing else could. Is it hard? Yes. Do you want it to be over? Sure. But just because you're in a rush for this season to end, don't neglect the lesson in it. Don't lose the value of it. God doesn't waste any moment of your life. He doesn't waste a hurt, tear, or bad situation. Does He cause it? No. But He will allow you to go through it and come out on top. He will deliver and see you through. He will carry you and use it for your good. He will restore everything that's been lost to you. Yes, you're tired and growing weary. But ask God for energy and strength to get through the rest of this journey. He will help you see the beauty in your test and storm. He will use and make your greatest pain your greatest blessing. Remember that.

Truth Verses: Romans 5:3, Galatians 6:9, Joel 2:25

Beautiful Truth

Day 159

And bigger doesn't always mean better. Today, work with the amount you've been given. There's a reason why God has given you what He has given you. There's a reason why He started you out in this manner and way. He has blessed you to do many great things. He's given you gifts and talents beyond measure. But that won't always equate to "big" in the beginning. Sometimes, you'll have to start off small. Sometimes, all you'll have is humble beginnings. And there's nothing wrong with that. That doesn't make you a failure or insignificant. It doesn't mean you won't amount to more and greater in the future. It just means this is where you are right now. Your life isn't over. This isn't "it" for you. This isn't the end. It's the beginning. Walk in it. There is greatness in your future. God has already declared the best for you. But right now is preparation time. Right now is sowing. Quit feeling bad about it. Quit thinking there's something wrong with you. There isn't. You're just fine. Excel with what you've been given and with what you've been blessed with. God will take care of the rest. He'll get you to where you need to be.

Truth Verses: Job 8:7, Ecclesiastes 9:11, Romans 12:3

Beautiful Truth

Day 160

If you were supposed to be like everybody else, God would've made you that way. But He didn't. He set you apart for a reason. Today, dare to be different. Stop being so quick to go with the crowd and to do what everyone else is doing. Do you honestly like the result everyone else is getting? Is that what you truly want to aspire to? If it is, then stay on the route you're on. Keep doing the things you're doing, hoping you'll arrive at the same destination as others. But if God has placed a different dream or vision in your heart, pursue it. Don't sit on it or hold back. Don't doubt and think it can't be done. Just because you haven't seen it done before doesn't mean it's impossible. Nothing is impossible with God. Just like He did for the Israelites, He'll part a Red Sea if that's what needed to get you to your destiny. Stop thinking about the "what-ifs" and what could go wrong. Yes, things could not turn out like you want them to. But what if they do? What if everything you're dreaming and thinking of is only a few steps away? What if things could really be different in your life? Get out there and find out. That's what faith does - it steps out. It pursues. You don't need faith to stay where you are. You know the fruit of that labor. Discover the fruit of a different labor. Find out what happens when you step out and go fully forward in God. You can make excuses all day. But if you want different, do different. Put your faith and action to work.

Truth Verses: Matthew 19:26, Exodus 14:21,
Romans 1:17, Hebrews 11:8 – 11

Beautiful Truth

Day 161

And you'll cross that bridge once you get to it. Today, stay in the moment. Stay right where you are. The opportunities and blessings God is providing for you aren't going away. What's yours is yours. God has already written and given it His stamp of approval. But the problem is you don't believe that. You think you must rush and get ahead of the plan to make something happen. But you don't. You're on God's timing. You're on His plan and way. The way the situation unfolds is going to be His doing, not yours. It's going to be up to God how it all shakes out. Stop racking your brain about it. This is why you feel stressed and uneasy. Real peace comes by allowing God's grace to flow in your life. It comes by giving your burdens over to God. It comes by stepping out of the problem and letting God take care of it. That's how you sincerely walk in the blessings of God - you allow Him to bring it all together without your worry or input. Stop putting the cart before the horse today. Refuse to jump ahead of God, trying to make plans where there are none right now. When the opportunity arises, just let it unfold. You don't have to make a decision or figure out what to do next. Ask God what needs to be done, then wait for the answer. It's that simple.

Truth Verses: 2 Corinthians 1:22, Proverbs 20:24, Psalm 68:19

Beautiful Truth

Day 162

When God says "no," it's not you He's rejecting. It's the plan you've selected for your life that isn't His best that He's rejecting. Today, separate yourself from the action. The enemy is good at making you think God doesn't like you, that He's always "picking" on you and that He never truly meets your desires. But that isn't true. Have you truly prayed, but never received anything from God? No. God hears and answers your prayers. But you're upset because what you want isn't what God wants for you. You're crying and throwing a fit, blaming God because the direction you have for your life is different than His. But you're pointing the finger at the wrong person, child of God. God is on your side. He loves you. He's not against you. He's always looking out for what's best for you. And because God loves you, He's not always going to give you everything you want, especially when He knows it's no good for you. That's what a good Father does - he protects. Just because other people haven't protected and cared for you in this way doesn't mean you get to say God is wrong and unfair to you. He isn't. He's protecting and keeping you safe under His wings. Stop fighting Him. Instead, ask God to change your heart, to remove all desires that aren't from Him. Tell Him you want His plans over yours. It's only when you surrender your wants that you'll be able to truly accept His. Remember that.

Truth Verses: Exodus 3:7, Psalm 84:11, Matthew 7:11

Beautiful Truth

Day 163

It's your thankfulness that moves God, not your complaints and grumbling. Today, be thankful in all things at all times. How? Get your mind off your problems. You can't be thankful going through the checklist of what you don't have and how unfair it is. You can't be thankful pointing your fingers at God, talking about what He's not doing. Shift your focus. Change it from what's wrong with everything and everybody to how blessed you truly are. Sure, you don't have everything you want yet in this life. Yes, you've had some unexpected, horrible tragedies that have happened. Nobody is discrediting that. It's been a lot. But are you completely falling apart? Has your world been that much turned upside down that God has forsaken you, not showed His favor or hand upon your life? Has He not done one thing lately that's been a blessing? He has. The fact you're able to move and breathe is a blessing. The fact that you have a family to complain about is a blessing. The fact that you have a job to despise is a blessing. Not everybody can say that. There are plenty of people who wish they could still hear a family member's voice or be asked to do one more thing at work. Not everyone has the things that you've been blessed with. Yet, you're seeing it as a problem. Stop it. Regardless of the situation, God still is good, even in this. He's still worthy to be praised. Stop thinking and talking about your circumstances so much and you'll see it. It's all about perspective. Change your perspective today and it'll change your life.

Truth Verses: Hebrews 13:15, 2 Corinthians 4:8, Jude 1:25

Beautiful Truth

Day 164

And the Lord is your good Shepherd. He leads you to plentiful pastures, not dried-up, dead ones. Today, recognize the God you serve. He is a God of more than enough. He is a God of goodness and mercy. He is one of the good guys. He's on your side. He's for you, not against you. He's not out to make you suffer or feel pain. He's not trying to make your life hard and miserable. Too often you have the wrong image of God. This is why you don't consistently seek and stay close to Him. You hear the scriptures and speak the verses, but you don't believe in your heart. It goes in one ear and out the other. You don't truly believe and accept who God is. You don't truly absorb His goodness and how much He loves you. If you did, you wouldn't walk around with doubt. You wouldn't waver from one minute to the next. You wouldn't let the circumstance shake you. Why? Because you'd know your God is bigger than any circumstance. He's greater than what you can see, feel or touch. He's an awesome Father. He never sleeps so He can watch over you. He never takes His eyes off you so that you can walk in peace. Count on that. Be sure of that. Nothing by no means shall hurt or harm you. The weapon may come, but it won't form against you because God is watching over your life. Remain confident in his protection today.

Truth Verses: Psalm 23:1, Psalm 121:3 – 5, John 10:14

Beautiful Truth

Day 165

And sometimes you must look backward to understand and remember how God has been consistently moving you forward. Today, don't forget where you came from. No, God doesn't want you stuck in the past or in a bad situation. But He does want you to acknowledge how far you've come. He wants you to see how far He's brought you. Why? So you can stop beating up on yourself for where you are now. You think you should be further along, not struggling with the same challenges that you did in the past. But the truth is you're dealing with these issues a lot better now than you did before. Things that used to shatter your whole world don't so easily anymore. Celebrate that. That's victory. Just because it's not leaps and bounds doesn't mean it's not progress. Nor does it mean that God isn't proud and doesn't see your growth. He does. God sees any step as progress. Even the smallest of steps are massive in His eyes. He knows how much it's taken for you to get this far. He knows how much hurt and pain you've had to endure to get to this place. Where you are now is no surprise or disappointment to Him. It's right where you're supposed to be. You're not moving too fast or too slow. Your entire life is a continual, ongoing process. You're not supposed to be a master at something overnight. You're not supposed to have it all together in a matter of months or years. Real change and growth take time. Quit trying to sprint through your life. Take a breath and stop to see the improvements you've made. Then, grow and develop as God wants you to. He's not in a rush. So you shouldn't be either.

Truth Verse: Deuteronomy 8:10 –11, Romans 8:1,
Ecclesiastes 9:11, Romans 5:3 – 5

Beautiful Truth

Day 166

A thousand may fall at your side, ten thousand at your right hand, but it shall never come near you. Today, just because something bad happened to somebody else doesn't mean it's going to happen to you. Stop thinking and accepting that. It's not God's truth. The enemy plants those seeds of fear and panic all around you every day. He plants them in the media, with your family and friends, and at your job. He even plants seeds at your church. He wants you to hear about the panic and fearful things happening in the world. He wants you to watch those sad and depressing stories. Why? So you can think "what if this happened to me?" And it can if you keep feeding on the fear and allowing it into your heart and spirit. That's how the enemy works – he gains access into your life through fear and panic. But he can't access what you don't give him the keys to. Quit feeding on the things of darkness. The Word says nothing by no means shall hurt or harm you. The Word says God will keep in perfect peace him whose mind is steadfast and trusts in Him. That means keep your mind on Christ. That means keep your mind on the Lord, not on what's happening in the world, the economy or on your job. Can you fix any of these problems or make them go away? No. Then, why are you meditating on them? Get them out of your head. Your job is not to ponder on negativity. Your job is to pray for others and focus on the goodness of the Lord. And you can't lift others up and think on Jesus when you're meditating on the things of this world. You can't help others if you're as shook up as they are. Dare to be different. Turn yourself away from the things of this world. Stay focused on the Lord. Then, you'll experience the peace and joy of God, the things He's promised to you.

Truth Verses: Psalm 91:7, Isaiah 26:3, Proverbs 4:25, Philippians 4:8

Beautiful Truth

Day 167

Yes, you love your family. But their struggles are not your struggles. Their battles are not your burden. Today, the closest thing to you could be the very thing holding you back. Yes, you care about your family and want to be there for them. But not if it's getting in the way of your own progress and success. Not if it's getting in the way of you receiving the things of God. The enemy knows how to distract you. He knows who to use to get you off course. So why wouldn't he use the ones you care about the most? Why wouldn't he make you become consumed with their problems and issues? Why wouldn't he make you feel guilty and condemned for wanting to pursue your own thing? It's the enemy's job to get in your ear like that. Quit being shocked and surprised by his tactics. Instead, recognize that you're not obligated to anyone or anything unless God tells you to be. It doesn't matter if it's your family or not. You've got to get to the things of God. You've got to live your life and do the things God is calling you to do. God isn't going to ask you about your loved ones and what they were supposed to do. He's going to ask you about you and what you did. That's what God is concerned about regarding you. He does care about your loved ones, too. But He must help them. You can't change or control what they do and how they do it. Give them over to God today. Let Him take care of their troubles. You? Continue to pray and intercede for them. That's what you've been called to do.

Truth Verses: Ephesians 5:31, Galatians 6:5,
Romans 14:12, 1 Timothy 2: 1 – 3

Beautiful Truth

Day 168

You have nothing to fear but fear itself. Today, God is not going to let anything happen to you. Stop being scared. That gut-wrenching, anxious feeling you're feeling, didn't come from God. It came from the enemy. He's responsible. He wants you to act on the fear he's giving you. He wants you to speak on it. He wants you up at night, pacing back and forth, losing sleep and time. Why? Because he's after your peace. He's after your rest. He's out to destroy you. Don't you know that? The enemy will not always come with some big problem or trial in your life. That's the thing he wants most is to throw you off course little by little. He knows there is no peace in fear. He knows there is no rest in worry. That's why he's attacking you so hard. Strike back. How? Declare God's protection over your life. That's how you combat fear. You get confident and speak that God's presence is all around you, that He is protecting and keeping you. Speak that. Speak that God is providing for you and that you're always on His mind. The enemy can't do anything with that type of confidence and belief. He can keep barking, but he can't bite. He has no power. He's defeated. Quit giving in to the anxiety he's feeding you. Stay close to God and watch the enemy flee from you on this day.

Truth Verses: Psalm 112:7, Proverbs 3:25 - 26, 1 Timothy 1:7, John 15:5

Beautiful Truth

Day 169

You're wonderful and amazing. You can do anything you put your mind to. But if you don't believe that, who else will? Today, it doesn't matter what anyone else says or believes about you. It matters what you believe about yourself. It matters what you see when you look in the mirror. It matters what thoughts you succumb to and what lies from the enemy you believe. God didn't create you to live and breathe for someone else. He didn't create you for approval or for someone to cheer you on all the time. He created you for His purpose. And because of that, you must be confident in who you are. You must know and believe you're a child of God, regardless of who's on your side or who says you can or cannot do something. Stop looking for someone to define you. Define yourself. Ask God who you are and who He's called you to be. Walk in it. Quit looking for others to dictate your identity and direction in this life. Your biggest enemy isn't everyone else. It isn't the people at work, the government or your family and friends. It's you. You're the only one that can make or break you. You're the only one that can stop your own progress. Don't look to put the accountability on other people. Believe God to validate you. Whatever it is He's assigned you to do, through Him and in Him, you can do it. Period.

Truth Verses: Philippians 4:13, Ephesians 2:10, Hebrews 13:21

Day 170

All roads don't lead to "yes." Sometimes, they lead to "no." Today, it's ok. In this life, you won't always get what you want. You won't always get the thing you're wishing and praying for. Sometimes, the very thing you're planning on, the one you're so sure of, doesn't work out. And when it doesn't, it's alright. It won't feel ok, but it is. Even in disappointment, there is still a plan. There is still goodness. God's hand is still at work. You're not supposed to understand it or "get it." You're just supposed to trust God. You're supposed to trust that whatever you wanted at this time wasn't God's best for you. Sure, it hurts. But God doesn't waste a hurt. Your tears are not in vain. Everything you're feeling right now, at this very moment, it's going to work together for your good. As hard as it may be, push past your feelings. Get out of the initial reaction of the disappointment. Get your mind focused on the truth of God's word. Keep your head held high. That's how you'll come through this trial. You may not know how and when, but be confident that it's all going to work out. It's all going to come together in your favor.

Truth Verses: Jeremiah 29:11, Romans 8:28, Psalm 30:11, Psalm 42:5

Beautiful Truth

Day 171

And yes, change is hard. But you must move forward. Today, you can't stay where you are forever. As comfortable and familiar as it is, that season of your life is over. God does everything in steps. He never takes you to a place you can't handle, and He never pulls you out from one when you're not ready. If He's nudging you to leave, it's because it's time. It's because you're truly ready. It doesn't matter what your friends say. It doesn't matter what your feelings say. It doesn't even have to make sense to you. You know the voice of the Lord. Follow it. Follow His instructions. Quit thinking about it so much. The more you think about the change you must make, the more hesitant you'll become. You'll find every reason under the sun to not go forward with the desire God has put in your heart. Fear will try to grip you. Don't let it. You have nothing to fear. God is for you. If this truly wasn't your time and season, He wouldn't have opened the door. But He did, so just walk right through it. Trust that now is the time. Trust that His grace and provision will show up where you need it most. You don't always have to know the "what" or the "why". All God needs you to do right now is walk. Walk right into what He has for you so you can have a fulfilled life, one you don't look back on in regret.

Truth Verses: Psalm 95:7 –8, Philippians 3:13 – 14, Isaiah 41:10, 2 Corinthians 9:8

Beautiful Truth

Day 172

And stressing yourself out about it isn't going to make the situation any better. You know what you must do. Do it. Today, pray about it. That's the answer to this problem and every other problem. Talk to Jesus about it. Quit trying to figure out this situation on your own. The truth is you honestly don't know what to do. You honestly don't know what's best right now. And that's ok. That's why you have a Savior. That's why you have the Holy Spirit. He knows what to do. He knows what's best in this situation. He sees the end from the beginning. Jesus knows why this situation is occurring and what it connects to in the future. He knows what's down the line. You don't. So you're just going to have to trust Him. You're just going to have to believe that God knows better than you, that if He brought this situation to you, He has an ultimate plan to get you through it. It's not to hurt or harm you. It's not to make things worse. God is always looking to elevate you, to make things better in your life. Stop thinking the worst. Honestly, stop thinking about the situation altogether. God's got this. Tell Him what your worries are. Tell Him how you feel about the situation. Tell Him that you don't know what to do, but you trust He'll tell you. Then, release it to Him. Your job is not to dominate and take control over what's going on. It's to release it to God. That's what serving Him is all about.

Truth Verses: John 16:13, Romans 8:26,
Proverbs 3:5, Matthew 11:29 – 30

Beautiful Truth

Day 173

And maybe you don't know who you really are because you've always tried to be someone else. You've always tried to be who people wanted you to be instead of being yourself. But you'll never be happy like that. Today, being you is ok. There's nothing wrong with you. Be the person God has called you to be. You don't have to fit into someone's little box or perfect picture frame of you. You don't have to fit some mold or prototype. God has never called you to be like someone else. You weren't born with someone else attached to your hip. You're fearfully and uniquely made. There is no other person like you on this earth. There is no one else who can do what you do. But if you can't figure out who you are, how will you know what to do in this life? How will you know what your purpose is? How will you manage your days? How will you know what to say "yes" and "no" to? How will you truly know what God is leading and guiding you to do? Stop idolizing and emulating other people, and you'll find out. Be ok with how you look, what you bring to the table and how God made you, and you'll see it. You can't experience unspeakable joy living out someone else's life. Find yourself. Ask God to help you start loving you, and to see all the great and beautiful things you have to offer. Ask Him to help you see your value and worth. Then, you'll experience true peace in your life, the peace that surpasses all understanding.

**Truth Verses: Jeremiah 1:5, Romans 8:30,
Psalm 139: 13 – 14, Philippians 4:7**

Beautiful Truth

Day 174

And it's not over. It's not over until God says it's over. Today, your best is still yet to come. Don't give up now because things have gotten hard. Don't throw in the towel because the heat is on. Yes, it is hard. Yes, the situation seems painful, unfair and unnecessary. It hurts. There's no doubt about it. But as much as it hurts, God's allowing you to go through it for a reason. Your trouble and pain is all working together in your favor. How? It's teaching you something, right? You're learning more about life and your relationship with God, right? You're learning more about what does and doesn't work, right? Well, then there's value in the problem. It doesn't feel good, but the best lessons in life sometimes bring the greatest pain. They illustrate that you don't know as much as you thought you did. They let you know you're truly not in control. They show you how to depend on God and not anyone else. As difficult as it may be today, keep pushing forward. Keep doing what you're doing. God isn't asking you to fake how you feel. You don't have to "tip through tulips" every day. That's not how this process works. Some days you'll feel like there's no hope or light at the end of the tunnel. There's nothing wrong with that feeling. That doesn't mean you don't have faith or that you've turned away from God. It just means you're having "a moment." God gets that. But let it be just that - a moment. Make it temporary. Don't live there. Don't allow that feeling to stay in your heart. Kick, scream and shout if you must. Sulk a little bit if need be. Then, pick yourself up and dust yourself off. You must get to the other side. Remember that.

**Truth Verses: Psalm 126:5 – 6, 2 Corinthians 4:8 – 9,
2 Corinthians 4:17, Luke 8:22**

Beautiful Truth

Day 175

And the minute you get out of the way is the moment God can do something. As long as you're standing there, trying to figure this thing out all by yourself, you'll always come up short. Today, God is the key to your breakthrough, not you. You're the one holding everything up. How? You're in the middle of it, trying to solve it and make God move on it. But God doesn't march to the beat of your drum. He marches to His. This is His plan. The truth is God has already moved on everything you could ever ask, imagine or dream of. It's finished. It's been created, said and done. But it won't manifest because you're in the mix of it. Take your hands off it. God doesn't need you constantly thinking and talking about it, or conjuring up some plan. Relax. Have trust in God to bring things together for you. Isn't that why you're praying to Him? Isn't that why you believe in Him? If you really could do all this by yourself, you wouldn't need a trusted Savior. But you can't. You need His help. Act like it. Let go of what you want. God has an ultimate plan and it's awesome. It's good and fitting for you. Let Him create this win for you. You'll be so much happier and better off. Watch.

Truth Verses: John 19:30, Psalm 37:5 – 6, Luke 22:42

Beautiful Truth

Day 176

And you're under the grace of God. That's why you see these miracles happening in your life. Today, quit thinking the goodness you're seeing has something to do with you. It doesn't. You're an imperfect creature. One day you have it all together and the next you don't. One minute you're praising God and the next you're cursing man. Every other second you mess up literally. But it's ok. God loves you anyway. He isn't keeping track or score of how many times you make a mistake in a day. So why are you keeping track of how many times others fall short? Don't you know that with the same measure of mercy and love He shows you, you should be providing it to others? His love isn't built on your performance or on what you do from moment to moment. It's built on Jesus Christ and His sacrifice. It's built on the fact that He said "yes" to God's plan so that you could have eternal and abundant life. Stop thinking your blessings are based on how "good" you've been acting. Stop making others believe that if they behaved like you, they'd receive the same thing. Life is not a classroom. You're not receiving better grades or higher marks because you passed all the tests. We all fall short of the glory of God. But by His grace, we all are saved. God wants everyone saved and in His presence. Just because this is your season of reaping doesn't mean you get to look down on others. God gives favor to whom He chooses. Everything you have is because of His goodness upon you. Come off your high horse. Be humble and acknowledge His grace in all your ways.

Truth Verses: 1 Corinthians 15:10, Romans 3:23,
Ephesians 2:8, James 4:6

Beautiful Truth

Day 177

Honestly, you have a lot to be grateful for. Can you walk and talk? Is your family ok? Does your car work? Did you get out of bed today? Did you have something to eat already? Were you able to go to work? If you said yes to any of those, then there's plenty you have to be thankful for. Today, there's way more for you than against you. Quit being so focused on the negative. Life is all about perspective and seeing the full picture, not just the bits and pieces. If you focus on what you're lacking and what isn't happening, you'll constantly be upset with God. You'll always think He's the ruler of Heaven and Earth, but He isn't doing anything for you. You'll always think God is looking to take things away from you. But that isn't true. God is always working on your behalf. Don't discredit what He has done for you just because He hasn't provided what you've been asking for. The enemy works overtime to lead you to that conclusion. He is the king of darkness and everything he has you focusing on will point to darkness, negativity, and defeat. He'll always tell you what's bad about the situation and what God isn't doing. Stop listening to the foolishness. You're letting the enemy speak way too much to you. Praise drowns him out. Thanksgiving gets him off your back. The truth is God is doing a mighty work in your life. Think about all the things you do have. Think about how safe and protected you have been. That's God's work. Your life isn't falling apart. You're blessed. That position and stance never changes. You're a child of God. Everything you need has been provided for. Be confident and grateful in that. Then, your perspective and everything else will line up accordingly.

**Truth Verses: Psalm 118:28, Deuteronomy 28:6,
1 Chronicles 16:34, Psalm 7:17**

Beautiful Truth

Day 178

Your moment to shine will come. But for now, celebrate someone else's. Today, the degree to which you honor another will be the degree to which you will be honored. Too many times when God blesses those around you, you can't be happy for them because you're thinking about yourself. You can't praise God for the work He's doing in their life because you're thinking "what about me?" Well, what about you? God hasn't changed His mind about you. He hasn't decided to take back His promises or blessings for you. You're still in line for them. But it's not your time yet. Contrary to your belief, it won't always be your time. It's not always about you. God is always using you to help someone else. That's how you remain humble and selfless. God isn't looking to promote you all the time. Sometimes He's looking to see if you can handle not being promoted, but can still praise Him and honor others. That's the type of person God can use. That's the type of person that cares more about God than themselves. That's who God needs in His kingdom, to fight the good fight. Learn how to be that type of person. Quit being the person with the wrong motives, always looking out for self. You're blessed to be a blessing. Everything you have is meant to be used and given away. Stop thinking it's for you and your gain. It's to bless and enhance the kingdom of God. Remember that.

Truth Verses: James 3:16, Philippians 2:3, Galatians 5:26, 1 Peter 3:8

Beautiful Truth

Day 179

Yes, things could be better. But it's not all bad. Your life is still good. Today, remember that. You can get so focused on the negative that it's all you see. You can forget how God has blessed you. You can forget the miracle He just provided to you. You can forget how He has continually brought you out of situations. Just because you're not where you want to be doesn't mean you're down and out. God still has His hand on you despite the circumstance. Stop murmuring and complaining. Don't you know every time you complain you set yourself back? Don't you know it's a slap in God's face? You're showing Him that you are more focused on your lack than His supply. You're showing Him that if things aren't going your way, you can't be happy. Stop living your life like this. The truth is on most days things will not go your way. But despite that, God is giving you grace. He's giving you the grace to handle it. He's giving you the grace to get through it with joy. Quit speaking and talking about how bad it is all the time. Sure, some things are frustrating. But you still serve a good God. He's still on the throne. And His goodness follows and chases you down wherever you go.

**Truth Verses: Psalm 78:11, 2 Corinthians 12:9, Psalm 100:5,
Psalm 23:6**

Beautiful Truth

Day 180

And you are who you say you are. If you say you're anxious and all worked up, that's exactly what you'll be. Today, stop speaking yourself into destruction. The enemy doesn't even have to do anything to you. Your words are doing enough. They are killing enough of your dreams. They are causing enough havoc. They are stopping enough blessings. You keep looking at God and everyone else, but it's you causing some of the damage in your life through your words. Your part is to speak life and to believe everything God has told you. Contrary to your belief, it's not your job to bring blessings to pass. It's not your job to make your life prosperous and abundant. It's God's. But you do have to agree with it. You do have to line up with it. And you line up with it by your words. Your words show what you truly believe. Show that you believe and agree with the things of God. Quit calling yourself dumb. Quit saying you're stupid. Quit speaking "I can't and I won't." You're a child of God. There's nothing you can't do. God is not only on your side, but He's all around you, working on your behalf, working for your good. You cannot lose. The fight and journey of your life is fixed. You're going to win. But the true test is in your mouth. You'll lose and keep losing every time if you don't get it together in that area. Remember that.

Truth Verse: Proverbs 13:3, Matthew 12:37, John 11:40, Romans 8:32

Beautiful Truth